There's Got to be More

Florence N Beukes

There's Got to be More

© Florence N Beukes, 2015

All scripture quotations are taken from the Amplified bible. Used by permission ©Zondervan, 1987. All rights reserved.

F. N. Beukes
P.O. Box 571
Rehoboth
Namibia

Email: beukesf7@gmail.com
Copyright 2015 Florence N Beukes

Cover Photography: Melba Van Wyk

Heaven Blessed Photography ©

Cover Design: Florence N. Beukes

All rights reserved. No part of this publication may be reproduced, in any form or by any means without the prior written permission of the Author and Publisher.

ISBN: 978-99945-79-40-2

Printed by Createspace, An Amazon.com Company

Dedication

I dedicate this book to all who hunger for a reality of Jesus Christ, His Kingdom and Glory. May you breakthrough into the unlimited as you search for 'More'.

Contents

1. *The Kingdom of God*................11
    i.   Seeking God first
    ii. The Kingdom of God
    iii. The Righteousness of God
    iv. Righteousness, Peace and Joy

2. *The Fire of God*................29
    i.   Purpose of the Fire
    ii. The Gift of Hunger
    iii. Witness to a dying world
    iv. Dig and keep on Digging
    v.   Quenching the Fire

3. *The Holy Spirit and Power*................47
    i.   A Kingdom of Power
    ii. Power birthed out of Love
    iii. Holy Spirit, Friend

4. Breaking Free..................................57
i. Dealing with Fear
ii. Dealing with Inferiority
iii. Breaking free from past hurt
iv. You have Gold

5. The Glory of God..............................76
i. There are Riches in Glory
ii. There is no effort in the Glory
iii. There is no distance in the Glory
iv. Carriers of Glory

6. Holy Desperation..............................93
i. Hannah's Desperation
ii. Jacob's Desperation
iii. The woman with the issue of blood

7. Heaven on Earth.............................107
i. The will of God on Earth
ii. Creating an Eden

iii. The mind of Christ
iv. What heaven on earth looks like

8. *Ruling and Reigning*............................*120*

i. Legislating from the courts of heaven
ii. How authority is gained
iii. Creation and Sound
iv. There's Power in your tongue
v. Living an ascended Life

9. *A Supernatural Life*..........................*142*

i.   An Open Heaven
ii. Wealth Transfer
iii. Dreams and Visions
iv. Keys to unlocking the Heavens

10. *It's all about Jesus*..........................*162*

i.   Loving Jesus
ii. Loving Jesus when it hurts
iii. Godly Encounters

Foreword

It is an honor to be able to write the foreword of the book; "There's got to be More." I hereby attest to the character of Florence Beukes whom I have known for over ten years in my capacity as her mentor. Florence is a talented musician, prophetic worshipper and leader in the ministry of God.

Her devotion to our Lord Jesus Christ testifies of her love for Him. This book is the first amongst many books to flow from her pen, and is birthed out of a desperate cry for more of God, His Kingdom and Glory. In July 2014, Florence was in a time of fasting and prayer which triggered the heavens to open up over her life. For four months, the Fire and Glory of God was poured into her and revelation knowledge was imparted which resulted in the writing of this book.

She continues to walk in God's Glory and ministers

from a place of intimacy with God.

I am convinced that this book will radically transform you, and launch you into a higher level of holy desire, intimacy and glory. All the Glory be to our Lord Jesus Christ, as He has made it possible for Florence to write on the amazing work God has done in her life, the miracles that followed and are still happening till this day.

To God be ALL the Glory!

Pastor A.J. Izaaks
Go Therefore Ministries
Rehoboth, Namibia

Chapter 1

The Kingdom of God

It all started with an extreme hunger for the reality of God and His Kingdom. I was not satisfied with my life as it was anymore. Living in poverty and struggling to get by was definitely not my portion. I had a business, but at times business was slow and that really frustrated me. My spiritual life wasn't really a fountain of paradise either. I was definitely not living a life of promise, success and prestige. Was this it? Is this the life I'm destined to live? How can I be a child of God and struggle all my life here on earth? Where was the glory upon my life? No! That is not my portion! Something had to happen. 'There's got to be more', I shouted. This can't be it!! There's got to be more!!

I was desperate for God and knew that wanting more or going deeper would cost me everything. Was I willing to pay the price? Well, at that time I didn't think of a price being paid. I just hungered for more of God. Little did I know that as the search for God continued how I had to give up everything if I wanted more; more of Him and less of me.

Now being a Christian for ten years already, and still not experiencing the promise of abundance and overflow was frustrating, until finally, I came to a place of desperation. I've quoted scriptures, fasted, prayed all night, half night, whole day, all that for years and never really lived an abundant victorious life. Now, I'm not throwing away ten years of Christianity. I went through some tough training over the years and it was not all bad. I was molded, shaped and melted again, over and over, probably a thousand times. It was necessary and beneficial, for myself and for God's Kingdom. Don't ever despise your wilderness training. Thank

God for it. However, some way or the other, things have got to change.

Let me ask you; "Have you ever started a business or any kind of career that somehow died? You tried to resurrect it without any success?" I was there, and I definitely wasn't planning on going on like that anymore. How about you prayed for someone where nothing instantaneously happened, and you just had to accept the fact that you were not really a Kathryn Kuhlman or John G. Lake? 'Was this normal living?' I would ask myself a thousand times. These were the questions that raced through my mind as I tried hard to keep my sanity intact. My frustration was not just material or financial instability; it was a search for both reality and purpose, in spirit, soul and body. Something had to be done. I needed answers, and very fast. The Holy Spirit started to deal with my heart as I embarked on this journey on "finding God". I soon realized that the pathway to the Glory of God is clear, but also very righteous.

Seeking God First

Mathews 6v33; *"But **seek** (aim at and strive after) **first of His entire kingdom** and His **righteousness** (His way of doing and being right), and then **all these things taken** together will be **given** you besides."*

So here I was, serving God now for ten years and going back to this scripture can be quite disappointing so to say. This scripture is kind of for 'new converts' we think. After their conversion we tell them, 'well, seek first the Kingdom of God.' I got that in the beginning of my conversion as well. 'You just seek God's Kingdom, forget about everything else', they would say. And when things get tough and you feel like quitting, they remind you once again, 'things will change, just keep on seeking the Kingdom'. I don't have a problem with talk like that. The only problem to me was, I'm seeking, I'm doing the right things, or was I? I realized later that I really didn't have a revelation of the Kingdom. A revelation of Jesus will change you. We sometimes build our lives on information based on what we hear, but revelation is what will bring about transformation.

This specific scripture clearly states that we have to *first seek* - *HIS KINGDOM*. You have to understand, that for you to know more about the Kingdom, you first need a relationship with the King of the Kingdom. Who is this King? His name is Jesus. The One who died and gave His life for you and me. Who, after three days, rose from the grave and is seated at the right hand of God Almighty. I'm talking about that King. He's the Lord of Lords, the All Sufficient One. King Jesus, our friend.

Now to seek is to be diligent and to be diligent is to be constant in effort. Was I really seeking God like that every day? I don't think so. To put God first is to boldly declare that He is your God. The first thing you ought to do when you wake up is spend time with Him, before you do anything else. First talk to God. First pray. So, seeking the

Kingdom first is to spend time with the King every day, to have that persistence no matter what, in pursuit of finding Him. The problem with us today, is that we are not really persistent. We do it for a month and then skip for a few days or even weeks, then we do it again, and we fall into this disheveled type of thing we call a relationship with God.

Let me tell you, it's not supposed to be like that. Christianity is to have that passion for Christ every day, to always be *in love*. Not just to pray every morning to keep the devil away kind of prayers, and then we just continue with our lives as usual. I was serious with my walk in God, but sometimes lacked that persistence in seeking Him. I had the presence of God upon my life, but lacked His Power and Glory. Sometimes frustration drives you against the wall, and you start to fast and pray, and for 2 to 4 weeks you feel good, but afterwards you find yourself back in the same old routine. You know what I'm talking about. Some of you are experiencing that right now.

Seeking God meant looking for Him with all my heart. It meant I had to lay down all my selfish desires. My ideas in exchange for His Mind. My dreams in exchange for His heart. My motives were dealt with day after day as I hungered for more of Him. We always say that finding God changes everything. Yes it's true, but seeking Him also changes everything. You are not the same as you journey up the mountain. The air gets 'thinner' the higher you go, so more stuff comes out of you that will cause you to be 'lighter' in a way. It is surprising to realize the baggage we still sometimes carry with us. To my experience I've had some really good deliverance sessions with God, no one who laid hands on me. The Holy Spirit kept dealing with issues in my heart I thought I dealt with a long time ago.

Your number one priority is to first seek God. A lot of people don't understand Kingdom and thus find it hard to really grasp the truth or reality of the concept.

The Kingdom of God

A Kingdom can be divided into two parts:

i). A King – The ruler (Highest authority) and,

ii). Domain – A territory over which rule or control is exercised.

The Kingdom of God is the Government of Heaven. Isaiah 9v6(a) records that;

*"For to us a Child is born, to us a Son is given; and the **government** shall be upon His shoulder, and His name shall be called Wonderful Counselor, Mighty God, Everlasting Father [of Eternity], Prince of Peace."*

What government? The kingdom of God. So, to have the Kingdom or Government of God in your life is to be completely submitted under His rulership. It means for God to completely reign in your life. No more your way of doing things, but having a blueprint from heaven on how to operate here on earth. No wonder we find Christians just doing their own thing and complain when they fail in their endeavors. We have to daily submit ourselves to His leading, to His authority. When the government of God comes into your life, *divine order* comes. *Divine alignment* comes. The government of God upon an individual or church brings a divine alignment and order. When divine order is restored, you begin to walk in the divine plan and purposes of God. Every individual, pastor, apostle etc., should have the Government of Heaven in their lives and ministry. It made me realize that even though I belonged to a church group, I myself needed to hear from God concerning my future and the plans He had in store for me. Thus, I had to walk in divine Government.

Every Government has laws. The law of the Government of Heaven is to Love God with all your heart and your neighbor as yourself and the 10 commandments will automatically not be broken. Yes, we live by grace and not under the law anymore. Grace is unmerited favor. It is to enjoy the blessings of God freely. Love is a free gift. So,

Love for God and your neighbor as yourself is the 'law' of the Kingdom of God. *James 2v8 says;*

"If indeed you [really] fulfill the royal Law in accordance with the Scripture, You shall love your neighbor as [you love] yourself, you do well."

To love is to obey. Complete obedience to God through love. Jesus said;

"If you [really] love Me, you keep (obey) My commands." (John 14v15), Also, *"If a person [really] loves Me, he will keep My word [obey My teaching]; and My Father will love him, and We will come to him and make Our home (abode, special dwelling place) with him" (John 14v23).*

So then, in the end, it's all about loving God, hearkening to His commands and loving others as yourself.

The righteousness of God

You have to understand that being righteous is to stand right with God. It is to be without sin, to hate what God hates. It also means to be holy. Now this is what we don't want to hear anymore. We don't want to listen to sermons on Holiness anymore.

We want to always hear that God will provide and bless us with the best and all that. Well, I am not against that, not at all. If there was someone who needed to hear that more, it was me. I just wanted God to bless me because I was sick and tired of struggling. Matthew 6v33 wasn't really what I wanted to walk in. I mean, I thought I was already living in His Kingdom and all that, but what struck me was the adding part. Where was the adding of my blessings if I sought the Kingdom? Why would God say seek first the Kingdom and His righteousness and all these things will be given you? Where were my blessings then? Why wasn't I living in abundance and overflow? I am living a holy life though. I wasn't drinking, smoking and doing all those nasty things. In fact, I went to church regularly, fasted now and then, prayed and really had a wonderful relationship with God, so I thought. The reality of God's Kingdom, invaded my life the day I got desperate for God. It really just shook me up to know that being righteous is to be so full of God that there will be no room in your heart and mind for sin. Is that even possible? Yes it is. Why would God say 'be holy for I AM holy?' Because He knows it's possible. It doesn't mean that you'll never get tempted. Oh no, you'll be tempted all right, but once the fires of righteousness start burning in you, it will be so much easier to say no to sin.

The purpose of John the Baptist was to preach repentance and righteousness to a lost and crooked generation. His role was to lead people into the kingdom or government of God, for their *'backbones'* to be restored. Prophetically the backbone symbolizes righteousness. I call every spiritual backbone into divine alignment, in Jesus name! Be straightened! You can pray like that over your church or your life.

The pathway to the Kingdom of God is a righteous path. You can't expect to move and live in His

Glory with sin in your heart. Whilst walking on that path, the fires of righteousness and purity will burn. After being baptized with the fire, holy living kind of became 'easier'. Suddenly I just wanted to spend more time with Jesus and the Holy Spirit. I just wanted to be in His presence. All of a sudden you no longer want to partake in worldly things. Christians ought not to make dirty jokes. It grieves the Holy Spirit. Ask yourself, is this thing I'm watching pleasing to God? Is what I'm saying pleasing to God?

How do I get to really be righteous? Spend time with Him. In spending time with Jesus or investing time, you will change. Your mind and heart will change. Secondly, ask Him to baptize you with His fire. Don't stop asking until the fire comes. Don't stop. That is what I did. I would cry out to God day and night for His fire. And when He comes, you'll know. The fire will consume you. At times you'll feel like it's just too much. This body cannot handle the fire, but *must* be purged. Young people everywhere, it's time to seek God, His Kingdom and Righteousness, and for His fire to fall on this generation. We need the fire!

Righteousness, Peace and Joy

It is written that;

"[After all] the kingdom of God is not a matter of [getting the] food and drink [one likes], but instead it is righteousness (that state which makes a person acceptable to God) and [heart] peace and joy in the Holy Spirit" (Romans 14v17).

As you seek God's Kingdom, righteousness, peace and joy will become evident in your life. These are the three pillars or characteristics of the Kingdom, the character of Jesus Himself. He is Peace, He is Joy and He is Righteous. Right-standing with God will birth peace in your life, and peace will establish joy. The one cannot be separated from the other. Peace and joy that you'll not be able to describe or comprehend. It is a peace not of this world. Peace means nothing missing, broken or lacking. Peace in your mind, heart, soul and body that will begin to overflow to the outside, influencing friends and family. Joy is a state of being content and satisfied. Joy is not based on your circumstances. Circumstances are subject to change, but joy must remain no matter the circumstances. Why? Because it's a state of being - in Christ. True joy is everlasting. It flows from the inside of us and not from buying a new house or car. Material things make us happy, which only lasts for a while. Happiness is temporal, joy is everlasting. The Kingdom in and around you will influence you and eventually change your circumstances. The reason why we struggle and stay stuck in the same situations or circumstances year after year, is because of a lack of Kingdom. I finally understood the dynamics of it all. As my relationship with God grew and my searching for the Kingdom, I began to change. My circumstances started to change, because my view of things changed. No wonder Jesus said, seek *first* the Kingdom. We ought to be rooted *in* the Kingdom and the Kingdom rooted *in* us.

We saw how Jesus, the Prince of Peace, calmed the storm when the waves were raging and rocking their boat. The disciples clearly had no peace in them, that's why they couldn't command the storm to subside. At times we too find ourselves in raging circumstances we can't control. We panic and run around looking for answers on the outside. When peace is evident in a Christian's life, he/she will not be intimidated by circumstances. You can only give what you have. How can we command storms to abate when we ourselves are full of fear and doubt? We ought to be rooted in Kingdom peace. The Kingdom is supernatural.

It is all through the Holy Spirit that we get to live a supernatural life. No Holy Spirit, no Kingdom life. The Holy Spirit is not to be excluded from the Kingdom. He is the one to lead and guide us. He is the one who teaches us about the Kingdom. I love how I can ask the Holy Spirit anything concerning Jesus and the Kingdom. He gives revelation and understanding. Love Him, cherish Him. He is our Friend.

Prayer

Dear Living Lord Jesus, I choose to submit myself under Your authority, Your rulership. Strip me from myself and my way of doing things. Change my heart, soul and spirit and fill me with Your love. Clothe me with grace to live and dwell in Your Kingdom. Show me Your ways, and usher me into the reality of who You are, in Jesus name.

Amen

Chapter 2

The Fire of God

There are numerous Christians out there who don't really know much about the fire baptism. We hear great men of God, talk on this subject, and we think it's just for them. It's for every Christian out there, whether in ministry or not.

John the Baptist stated that;

"I indeed baptize you in (with) water because of repentance [that is, because of your changing your minds for the better, heartily amending your ways, with abhorrence of your past sins]. But He who is coming after me is mightier than I, Whose sandals I am not worthy or fit to take off or carry; **He will baptize you with the Holy Spirit and with fire"** *(Matthew 3v11).*

Being baptized with the Holy Spirit in the evidence of speaking in tongues is wonderful. We find, in the book of Acts, that the apostles were gathered in one place, waiting on the promise of the Holy Spirit. They prayed for days and when the Holy Spirit suddenly showed up, they spoke in other tongues. But something else also happened on that day of Pentecost. Tongues of *fire* settled on them. I believe they were baptized with the Holy Spirit *and* Fire. I became hungry for the Fire of God. I wanted that, and also, to be as bold as Peter was when the Holy Ghost came upon him. I have found that boldness comes from being filled with the Holy Ghost. Not being afraid of what others will say and think of you anymore when you witness to them about Jesus. Boldness is what we need. I started praying for a baptism of the Holy Ghost and fire. I wanted the fire part. That is what was missing in my life.

Fire comes when there's a sacrifice. I've believed that to be completely true. Remember the prophet Elijah in the book of Kings, how the fire fell on the sacrifice? That's what happens with someone who is completely submitted to God, crying out for His Fire. The Fire will surely invade your life and utterly change you. Oh, the peace that floods your soul when the Spirit of God takes over. Cry out for a fire baptism. You'll never be the same again.

The Purpose of the Fire

The Purpose of the Fire is to purify, sanctify and consecrate you. It is also to anoint you for ministry. To purify is to cleanse or free you from anything that pollutes or contaminates you. It is to be refined or purged, like gold or silver is refined in a furnace. God wants us to be clean so He can inhabit us. He frees us from guilt and condemnation. We are consumed, spirit, soul and body.

I asked for a baptism of the Holy Ghost and Fire. We sometimes miss the fire part. Fire is symbolic of the presence of God, and is significant in the life of a believer. We need His presence every day.

We can't do anything without His presence. Moses encountered God's glorious presence through the burning bush experience. That fire encounter changed Him and set Him on a journey of redemption, for himself and a nation.

Before Esther's enthronement as Queen, she underwent beauty treatments. For six months she was bathed in spices and frankincense. That was her being deeply cleansed from the inside out. Her flesh was 'killed'. *The fire kills us*, from our way of thinking, from our fleshly desires. For us to breakthrough in Glory we have to be bathed in the fire. There is no other way.

The Fire of God preserves the flesh. Fire is like salt. It preserves you. Daniel and his friends were preserved in the furnace. A fourth man was seen in their midst. Jesus the ultimate, supreme fire preserved them from literal destruction or 'burn up.' The fires of this world cannot destroy you as you are flooded with God's fire.

The fire of God births Holiness. To be holy is to be 'set apart'. God's desire is for us to be 'set apart' for Him, for Kingdom purposes. It is written, *'Be holy, for I am Holy.'* He is coming back for a holy bride; A bride without spot or wrinkle.

The fire is a love baptism. It changes the way you think, act and respond to humans as well. You just begin to love more. Love burns. Love and fire cannot be separated. You'll never find cold love. Love is a heat wave. One of the scriptures I would continually pray was Ephesians 3v19 where the apostle Paul said;

"That you may really come to know [practically through experience for yourselves] the love of Christ which far surpasses mere knowledge [without experience]; that you may be filled [through all your being] unto all the fullness of God [may have the richest measure of the divine Presence and become a body wholly filled and flooded with God Himself]"

It is just amazing how the word becomes alive once you really tap into it with your whole being. I want the Holy Spirit to stay, to linger. I wanted to be full of God. Paul must've experienced it; otherwise he wouldn't have mentioned it. People always want to walk in greater power, yet never want to walk in holiness. The standard for going to heaven is still the same today - holiness, righteousness and purity. There's no other way. God is Holy. He is a consuming Fire. Deut. 4v24 says,

"For the Lord your God is a consuming fire, a jealous God".

He is Holy. He is Love and love burns. There is no sin in Him. We need the Fire of God to purge us from all sin. Do you want to be part of that Holy Bride? Then you have to burn. Allow God through His Spirit to cleanse you from the inside out. Ask Him to come burn in you. Prayer keeps the fire burning. You cannot be a Christian and not pray.

I remember, how in the beginning, when the fire came, how I would at times just cry. I was under so much conviction. I repented and cried and repented and cried. Oh, the Holy Spirit would just move on me so gently. My desire was to please Jesus and love Him. My perspective changed, my heart changed. I just loved people more. You will begin to consider other people and think before you speak. You find Christians just speaking their mind wherever they're at. Telling you they're just like that. Well, we ought to repent and ask God for His fire to fill our lives. We need more holiness sermons preparing people for the coming of the Lord. That is the only way to get into heaven, once you've surrendered your life to Jesus Christ.

Jesus is the doorway to the Father. Being a Christian is not enough, holy living should follow. We must live holy lives. Too many man-made things came into the church. We have all these beautiful names for sin. Sin is sin. We need to repent and live right. Preachers, you need to preach it like it is. Don't be afraid, but ask God for the fire and conviction to fall on the people. The fear of the Lord must return. How will it return if we don't pray and preach it like it is? Pray and prepare people the way Jesus wants it to be done. Lay down your way of doing things and ask God for His Kingdom to invade your life and the church. Revival will come when we pray and seek God.

The Gift of Hunger

Why am I referring to being hungry as a gift? I am talking about the lovesick longing for *more* of the One who is infinite. Hungering after God will usher you into a dimension of heavenly bliss. It is a gift to be treasured, for those who hunger, will be satisfied. Matthew 5v6 says;

"Blessed and fortunate and happy and spiritually prosperous (in that state in which the born-again child of God enjoys His favor and salvation) are those who hunger and thirst for righteousness

(uprightness and right standing with God), for they shall be completely satisfied."

Every promise in the word of God is yes and amen. When He says you'll be satisfied, you will be, that is, if you *hunger*. We find so many Christians, hungry for fame, money, power, acceptance and much more. These things will never satisfy you. Satisfaction comes merely from God and Him alone. I know of people who have practically everything they want, yet lack peace and joy. Why is that? Because they don't have God. You can buy another car, house, get a bigger wallet, but I'm telling you, you'll always be looking for something more. When you hunger for God, He will satisfy you. Of course there's no problem in buying houses or cars or whatever it is you want. The point is that contentment comes purely through a relationship with Jesus Christ. Start by asking for more of Him. He will never disappoint you.

After extensive times of fasting and prayer, I would go out and pray for people. We started a hospital ministry where once a week, we'd pray for the sick. We would preach and lay hands on the sick according to Mark 16v18, and we would see healings take place and people touched by the Holy Spirit. But still, I would come back home and cry out to God for more. Somehow, I just wasn't satisfied with that. Yes, thank God for that anointing, but I wanted more. There had to be more to it than this. I believe there are depths in God we've never even experienced before. Realms of reality we've never even entered. Why should we be satisfied when there is more? It's got nothing to do with being ungrateful. No. It's appreciating what God gave you, but hungering for more. There's nothing wrong with that. In fact, God loves it when we want to go deeper and higher. So, even when you walk in a level of the anointing, or the fire, there's more. I asked God to increase the fire in my life. I don't think I had any idea what I really asked for. At times it would be so much that some nights, I couldn't sleep. I would burn with intense heat. My whole body would be saturated with His fire. I felt like dying at times. It would be more than I could handle, I thought, but God would give me the grace to handle it. Then I started seeing all kinds of miracles, short legs growing, backs straightened, infected lungs healed etc., and I realized that there was power being imparted. It made me think on how Jesus said the Holy Ghost will come on you and you shall receive power to be effective witnesses, (*Acts 1v8*). I told God that I wanted to be an effective witness, and that I needed His Power. The more I prayed for Kingdom Holy Ghost Power, the more I would burn. They say everyone's experience is different. I believe so. To me I would burn with fire! Demons would come out more easily by not having to shout or even pray half a day. In one month I saw short legs grow and people getting healed now more than I could ever imagine. It was overwhelming, yet remarkably exceptional. No longer was the Fire just inside of me, it was now flowing through me.

Witness to a dying world

God wants us to minister to a dying world. It's all for His Kingdom. Four months into seeking God and the fire would just burn. I've found myself not being able to sit and be still anymore. The fire will cause you to go out there and tell people about Jesus. God wants a people who will bring in the harvest. The harvest is ripe. Laborers arise with fire in your bones! People say, 'well, that is just not my ministry, I'm not an evangelist.' Me neither. I'm in the prophetic, yet we have a command to go out into the entire world and preach the Gospel.

Not everyone is cut out to host crusades, but you can start by witnessing to the people at your workplace, at school even, wherever you are. You cannot be on fire and not talk about Jesus. Start by telling your cousins, friends, boss or even your teacher. I was actually a very shy person at first, but when the Holy Spirit got a hold of me, boldness stepped in. The way you sing, walk, talk, preach, teach and prophesy will change. Whatever it is, it'll change. Like with Peter, after he got baptized with the Holy Ghost and fire. He just wasn't the same person. The apostles had a newfound boldness and brashness, through the Holy Spirit, that catapulted them into the ministering of the gospel.

Start praying for a baptism of the Holy Ghost and Fire. Don't stop until it happens, (*Matthew 7v7*). One of God's generals and Fathers of Faith, John G. Lake, would pray and pray and not stop praying for the baptism of the Holy Ghost until He came. He was used in mighty revivals in Africa and across the world. He would be so full of fire that even deadly viruses would die in his hand. Thousands of people got saved under his ministry. The apostles themselves never kept silent. They preached the word. I mean, they would be persecuted, but kept on preaching. Do your colleagues even know you're a Christian? Some of you have been working that job now for years and no one really knows you're born again. It's time to change. It's time to take a stand.

Dig and keep on Digging

I mentioned earlier on the importance of asking God and to keep on asking. Yes, for some, it might take longer than others, but what I've learned, is that while asking, God changes you. It's not like nothing happens. People tend to give up too easily. You might feel like God doesn't hear you or that He will never come through for you. He will come through for you if you don't stop asking.
Matthew 7v7 says;

"Keep on asking and it will be given you; keep on seeking and you will find; keep on knocking [reverently] and [the door] will be opened to you."

Don't be discouraged. Keep the faith. The key is to *keep on*. God is no respecter of persons. He is ever true to His promises.

In Luke 18, Jesus told the apostles a parable on

how to pray, that they must always pray, and not give up. He said that there was a certain judge in a city, who didn't fear God, neither had respect for man. A widow would often go to him to defend her case. This judge just didn't care, he refused to help her. And this widow would just keep on coming back to the judge in hope that he would change his mind. However, after some time he grew tired of her continuous effort in pleading with him. He said,

*"Yet because this widow continues to bother me, I will defend and protect and avenge her, lest she give me intolerable annoyance and wear me out by her **continual coming** or at the last she come and rail on me or assault me or strangle me" (Luke 18v5).*

I'm not implying you should beg God to give you something. No. If this unrighteous judge could decide to help this widow, how much more a loving God? This widow's longevity caused her to breakthrough. I've learned to be persistent in asking. It's like digging for gemstones. You won't find them on the surface of the earth. You'll have to dig and dig. So that when you finally find the treasure, you'll learn to appreciate it once you have it.

Quenching the Fire

The fire can and will be quenched when you allow sin in your life. If you find yourself sinning, repent and stop   doing what you did that was wrong. The key is to stop doing it and not to continue. You can't keep on feeding the flesh. Feed your spirit with the word and prayer. Fuel the fire with prayer. Only prayerful Christians will be hot. If you don't pray, you'll die spiritually.

I know of people that are just satisfied with their Christian lives as it is. They enjoy church, fellowship with the brethren and go to work every day, just the usual routine of life. As long as they're not moving out of their comfort zones they're fine. Is this the life you want to live for the rest of your life? Don't you want to go higher and deeper in God? Are you really happy? I mean really happy? We should never feel like we've arrived. There's more for us, so much more. It's time to dig deeper.

Prayer

Oh Father in Heaven, in the name of Jesus Christ, Baptize me with the Holy Ghost and Fire. Burn away the dross in me. Purge my mind, my heart, my soul and body in Jesus name. Oh Lord, let the fires of righteousness burn in me. Straighten my backbone and restore divine order and alignment in my life, in Jesus name! Baptize me with Your liquid love. All consuming fire, come burn in me!

Amen

Chapter 3

The Holy Spirit and Power

When I first became a believer, my mentor would teach me about the Holy Spirit. I loved those sessions on the Holy Spirit. I learned that He is not an 'it' but a person. He is a Supernatural Being, He is God. Yes, He is. Not *like* a God, but He *is* God – God the Holy Spirit. I cultivated a relationship with the Holy Spirit and He became my friend. I would talk to Him daily; ask Him questions concerning the bible and Jesus. It's just an amazing journey once you really let the Holy Spirit lead you into all truth. Somewhere along the line, like many of us, we become content.

The power of the Holy Spirit is the power of God. The Spirit, the third Person of the Trinity, has appeared throughout Scripture as a Being through and by Whom great works of power are made manifest. His power was first seen in the act of creation, for it was by His power the world came into being. The Holy Spirit also empowered men in the Old Testament to bring about God's will;

*"Then Samuel took the horn of oil and anointed David in the midst of his brothers; and the Spirit of the Lord came **mightily** upon David from that day forward. And Samuel arose and went to Ramah" (1 Samuel 16:13).*

Jesus did say that the Holy Spirit will come on you, and you'll receive power. As I read these scriptures, I wondered where the power was. Why didn't I walk in this power? I had a baptism of the Holy Ghost. Where's the power then, I would repeatedly ask God. I would keep on asking God for a power baptism. I wanted to walk in the power that Elijah and all the other great prophets walked in. Have you ever prayed for someone and told them about the healing power of God and when you finished praying, the person was still in pain?

And then you pray again and again. I really hated that. It was unacceptable. I mean to pray for someone and nothing happens? That is not how I'm supposed to live. I'm a Supernatural being serving a Supernatural God who has Supernatural Power. I wanted the power. I just couldn't handle being powerless anymore.

A Kingdom of Power (Dunamis)

Dunamis is the ability and might of God. It is the ability to perform anything, not just power capable of anything, but power in action.

The Kingdom of God is a Kingdom of Power according to 1 Corinthians 4v20;

"For the kingdom of God consists of and is based on not talk but power (moral power and excellence of soul)"

During His earthly ministry, Jesus was filled with the Holy Spirit, led by the Spirit and empowered by the Spirit to perform miracles. After Jesus ascended to heaven, the Spirit also equipped the apostles to perform miracles. The power of the Holy Spirit was manifest amongst all the believers of the early church through the dispensation of spiritual gifts such as speaking in tongues, prophesying and much more. Jesus was full of the Spirit and Power.

I wanted to be full of the Spirit and Power. As I continued to pray for weeks, the Holy Spirit touched me. The electricity I felt. My body would vibrate under the power of God. Gentle vibrations of holy ecstasy. It was an incredible experience. What happened to me was an experience that cannot be described with words. You have to experience it to really understand.

There is a well of power inside every Christian that must be stirred up. I found that praying in tongues or in the Spirit, is one of the keys to tapping into that well of power. But be reminded that everything flows out of a relationship with Jesus. Also, we have to understand that power will not be given to anyone without a purpose. What is it you want do with power? Do you want to show off or be a true vessel of honor for God? Can He use you? Or flow through you to accomplish HIS purposes? As you begin to walk in the Kingdom, you realize that the Kingdom is a Kingdom of supernatural power. *It is the ability of Heaven.* It really bothers me that we are so ignorant concerning Kingdom Power. We need the power of God in this earth. Every day, we are faced with challenging situations which we can't handle because we lack the power in our lives. Please know, that the power of God is available to every believer, whether housewife, janitor, accountant or pastor.

The purpose of the King is to win back His bride. To gather souls for Him. Yes, the power is to destroy the enemy's plans. Yes, it is to heal the sick and drive out demons. It is to live a victorious life! By doing all that, you represent the King and His Kingdom. That is the purpose of Power. First to love. God's desire is for us to be full of love. Power is Love. It took me a really long time to grasp that. How can it be love? I thought it was the enablement to be an effective witness. Of course it is. Power is full of Love.

Power birthed out of Love

As you begin to grow in your love for God, you realize that love is the incubator for power. The two cannot be separated. I've learned that in the Kingdom, all things flow together in harmony. I began to see a different side of God I never knew. I knew God was love, we all know that, but praying Ephesians 3v19 completely changed my whole way of living.

That I may be filled and flooded with *Power* Himself, with *Love* Himself, with *Glory* Himself. So, to be so full of God actually means to be so full of His Love that demons flee. To be so full of His Glory that anything is possible. Are we this full of God? Are we so full of Love? So here I was, once again, falling to my knees, crying out to God for a baptism of Love and Power. Although I longed for the power of God, I understood now more than ever, that Dunamis *is* a fusion of *Love* and *Power*.

How can you walk in absolute power and not love? How can you walk in absolute Love and not have power to raise the dead? Well, it didn't matter anymore. What mattered most was that I be so full of God. Of course God wants us to have power. Yes, He wants us to be victorious. The deeper you go the more you love. The more you love, the more *powerful* you become. All this comes from a secret place of intimacy with God.

I began seeing more miracles. There were more healings now. More words of knowledge, more prophecies. It was great, but, there had to be more! A more effective way of ministry, a higher level. I realized that God alone is my satisfaction. But the more you find, the deeper you want to go. When you find yourself at this juncture in life, keep on pressing on. Don't stop!

Holy Spirit, Friend

The Holy Spirit is such an awesome friend. He will always escort you deeper into the Glory; because

He knows that there are depths to God we've never even touched before. That's why we ought to cultivate our relationship with the Holy Spirit. He is the one I always complain to, talk to and cry to. I can just be myself with the Holy Spirit. He is not just there when I minister, but He's there every minute of every day. If you want more of Jesus, you got to start developing your relationship with the Holy Spirit. Ask Him to read the bible with you, to give you revelation. He is our helper.

As children of God, we delight in what the Holy Spirit desires, we are now controlled, not by our old sinful nature, but by the Holy Spirit. The Spirit of Christ who dwells in us guarantees that He will raise us up on the last day, and even now by the power of the Spirit of God we can put sin to death daily. The Holy Spirit guides us in the way of righteousness. This Spirit is the Spirit of our adoption as sons of God and by Him we boldly cry, "Abba, Father." The Holy Spirit witnesses to our spirits that we are children of God, heirs of God and joint-heirs with Christ. He is the one to lead you into more of God!

Prayer

Sweet Living Lord Jesus, take me deeper into Your Love. Flood me with Your power, flood me with Your love. Take my life Oh God, and use it to bring glory to Your name. Oh Holy Spirit, lead me into all of God. Clothe me in Kingdom power, in Jesus name.

Amen

Chapter 4

Breaking Free

As I started to go deeper in God, I had to deal with some issues of my heart. My desire was to breakthrough and then He showed me how I allowed fear to block me from moving into greatness. No! I couldn't possibly be having fear? I thought. The truth is I did have fear. Fear of failure, fear of man; fear that I'm not good enough. Those were the things I thought I dealt with years ago.

Going higher up the mountain, deeper into the glory, will cause some deep hidden, sub-conscious issues to arise to the surface. We think we're fine. We forgave. Oh yes, we did. We moved on. With God nothing is hidden and when you allow Him, He will deal with you whether you bleed all over again. He'll deal with you until you're whole.

Because that's His nature; completeness and wholeness. He wants us to be confident and be at peace.

Dealing with Fear

Now, some might have had past traumatic experiences, which resulted in you hiding from the world, too afraid you might get hurt or rejected again. I urge you to seek help from a counselor, a close friend or spiritual leader. You have to let go of past pain and hurt. Yes, I know, it's painful at times, but the enemy wants you to hide. He doesn't want you to break free and become the real you, that God created you to be. God has placed so much in you, but, un-dealt fear will cause every gift inside of you to be locked up.

I had fear issues, which was not easy to admit but it's true. Here I was, a worship leader, ministering through song and also prophetically, which is my call, and now I had to actually realize all over again that I had to really, really deal with issues of fear. Perhaps you're struggling with the same things I struggled with and some may have other struggles. I'm not just referring to fear of dogs, lions, the dark etc., but also fear of the unknown, fear of man, of what they might say or think of you. It is vital for us to deal with all kinds of phobias if we want to go deeper. Throughout the bible, God would always command us not to fear. Do not fret or be anxious for nothing. Trust God to take care of you. He will never let you down.

Perhaps you're afraid to propose to the love of your life. Well, deal with it, and take that step. She's probably wondering when you're going to make a move. Are you afraid of ending up alone? Talk to God about that and ask Him to present someone in your life. You still have to make the choice yourself. You're probably called into full time ministry, and you're afraid of the unknown, how it's going to be, whether you'll make it or not. If God called you, He will guide you. He will provide and take care of you. Don't be anxious. What are you waiting for? Time is running out you know. Start that business you always wanted to. Take that trip you have planned now for years. Step out of fear as you step into Love.

Fear and faith are opposites, but for us to cross over from fear to faith, we have to deal with doubt. Fear kills faith. Fear will always cause you to doubt in the faithfulness of God. No wonder God throughout the bible, commanded us not to fear.
Fear is of the devil. There is no fear in God. He is perfect Love. Perfect Love drives out fear. 1 John 4v18 says;

"There is no fear in love [dread does not exist], but full-grown (complete, perfect) love turns fear out of doors and expels every trace of terror! For fear brings with it the thought of punishment and [so] he who is afraid has not reached the full maturity of love [is not yet grown into love's complete perfection]"

God is not out to punish you. He loves you. He wants you to be totally and completely free of fear. Renew your mind through the word. There is a statement that says; Fear is False Evidence Appearing Real. The enemy wants you to think that it's the real thing. It's not. It's false evidence. Stop believing what the enemy show you and start trusting in God. Everything He does is real. He is real and can be depended upon. Build your faith through the word, read it, think it and speak it.

It is of utmost importance that you deal with issues of fear, as it will cripple you and leave you numb.

Dealing with Inferiority

The Lord started to talk to me about recording my Album. I realized that I never really had the confidence in doing that. I have to admit, that it was actually the result of low self-esteem. I had an inferiority complex, which is a lack of self-worth. I was just satisfied with singing here and there. People would always ask me about my album and I would always say 'well, next year I suppose'. And so the years went by. Let me ask you this. What is it you have that you can do very well, and you lack the confidence to do it; because you think it won't be good enough? Or you just think people won't like it? I lacked confidence so I just never did it. When I started to contend for the glory, God talked to me on these issues. I wasn't planning on recording albums, writing books or movie scripts. All I wanted was to shine in the not so bigger crowds. So here I was, finally having to face my giants.

In Numbers 13, God spoke to Moses to send out men, that they may spy out the land of Canaan. They were to check out the land, whether the people who dwelt there were strong or weak, the estimation in population, how the economy was and whether it was a really good place to live in. Unfortunately, as it may be, these men came back with a very negative report. As they returned from their journey, they reported back to Moses and the entire congregation.

"We came to the land to which you sent us; surely it flows with milk and honey. This is its fruit. But the people who dwell there are strong, and the

cities are fortified and very large; moreover, there we saw the sons of Anak [of great stature and courage]" (Numbers 13v27, 28).

So what actually happened is that Caleb requested they go and possess the land. But the men who went with him said, no, they are not able to go up against the people, for they were stronger. They were so afraid and lacked esteem. As a result, unbelief and doubt crept in their hearts and crippled them of ever conquering the land. Caleb on the other hand, was confident and knew that all things were possible with God. The rest had no faith at all. They said;

*"The land through which we went to spy it out is a land that devours its inhabitants. And all the people that we saw in it are men of great stature. There we saw the Nephilim [or **giants**], the sons of Anak, who come from the **giants**, and we were in our own sight as **grasshoppers**, and so we were in their sight" (Numbers 13v32(b), 33).*

Notice how they perceived of themselves.

Proverbs 23v7 (a) records that;

"For as he thinks in his heart, so is he."

I mean, they were probably very excited at first, when they journeyed to this great land they most definitely only heard of. As they were on their way, they probably talked about how finally they were going to live in the land that God promised to their forefathers. What a shocker it must have been for some, to have come this far, only to realize that they actually didn't have it in them to overpower these giants. They thought of themselves that way. Their thinking stopped them from even 'trying' to fight. These were not just ordinary, church going brothers that were sent out. No. They were the heads or great leaders of Israel. They must've been really grounded in the word.

People looked up to them. They felt so inferior and insecure; they started seeing themselves as mere grasshoppers. Inferiority will cause you to perceive less of yourself. Do you at times feel like that? The first step to recovery or deliverance is to always acknowledge or admit that you have a problem. Denial will keep you rooted in whatever you're struggling with.

Here you are finally taking the step to make things happen, whether it's a new job, a new ministry, moving to Africa, or whatever it is you want to do. All of a sudden, while you're at it, you decide it's too hard or difficult to do it. Suddenly you see pastors or evangelists out there, really going all out for God, and you're not so sure of yourself anymore. You find students at campus complaining about chemistry or a lecturer, and you don't think you can do it. You see top businesses and just don't think you'll make it in the industry. You hear other people sing and you just don't think your voice is that good. All you see is how you're going to fail and before you even try it, you quit. All you saw was the impossibilities. Countless Christians are like that. You're probably one of them. I was one of them. You might say, 'well, I'm just not as gifted as the others', or, 'I don't have the money to do this or that', or, 'I will be rejected, I can't do it.' Don't sell yourself short. How long is this going to continue? Put your faith in God. He will be with you, as you will be successful. Without pursuing these creative endeavors, we risk living a meaningless existence, one which is sure to deeply affect our happiness and well-being.

As I was dealing with all this, the Holy Spirit led me to the scripture in the book of Samuel where David decapitated Goliath's head. He revealed to me why it was necessary to cut off Goliath's head. Not just because he wanted to prove to everyone including King Saul that Goliath was really dead. Now we know that, Goliath was a giant, a Philistine, who would come out morning and evening, scaring the Israelites with big talk, *(see 1 Sam 17).*

The Israelites felt intimidated by his gigantic looks and insulting remarks. After forty days of non-stop fear tactics, David, son of Jesse, finally stepped up and killed Goliath. Why cut of his head? Head symbolizes leadership/headship. David made a bold statement that no longer was fear and inferiority going to *rule* over them. Goliath no longer had control over them. Fear and inferiority no longer told them they were not good or brave enough. Fear and inferiority was completely silenced and dealt with. For too long we've allowed fear and inferiority to rule over us, as we listened to it talk us into backing down. No more! Cut of its head and let the headship of Christ lead you into victory!

Breaking free from past hurt

As a child, I grew up under a dark cloud of abuse, and this violation caused tremendous heartache over the years. It somehow shaped me into a shy, fearful and inferior person. I wasn't the person God created me to be. When I accepted Jesus as my personal Lord and Savior, things didn't change overnight. I had to unwrap layers and layers of pain and hurt to be healed. I had to forgive if I wanted to be free, and it certainly wasn't easy. Somehow, as I searched for more of God, He showed me how I still needed to deal with what happened years ago. I thought I already dealt with that, but hadn't really let go of a victim mentality. I made a choice to move forward. I forgave….again, and broke free from a cage that I was confined to for years.

Forgiving others sets you free. It's liberating. I asked God to bathe me in His Love and to make me whole again. I had to make a conscious choice to break free; you perhaps have to make that same choice today. Yes it's painful at times, but with Jesus all things are possible. Unforgiveness will cause you to be stuck, not moving into all that God has for you. I've been falsely accused, misunderstood and stabbed in the back by brothers and sisters, family and friends, but have had to forgive and move on.

You probably went through that as well. Make a decision. Forgive. Let go and let God take over. You'll find yourself soaring in and with Love as you unlock the padlock from your heart. You have the key in your hand, a key to freedom. If perhaps, you have caused pain in someone else's life, you have to make right. You're probably afraid to face that person, well, writing a letter is a great place to start. You'll never know how much it will mean to the person you've hurt. Your joy lies in forgiving others, yourself and making right with others.

As I read on the life of Joseph, I saw an example of endurance, forgiveness and love all displayed in one man. He was human just like you and me. He too had to forgive and soar above rejection, humiliation and false accusation. He probably had reason to quit and give up, yet Joseph never lost sight of a God who loved him, despite all the pain he went through. Are you hurt and feel like the world is against you? Turn to God. He is your healer, your deliverer, your strength. Allow Him to heal your heart and change you into a loving, forgiving person. You deserve to be free. Take that step to forgive, even if it's a tiny step. That's a great start!

You have gold

I once saw a map of Africa and on it were the different countries of course, but, what caught my attention was that every country's resources were showcased. Namibia, my country, had diamonds, zinc and I think copper in it. All of these countries displayed their main resources that country was rich in. Some were known for their oil, others for gold and so forth. So the Lord started to speak to me and He said that just as God has given every country resources, He has also given each one of us gold on the inside. We are the ones sitting on our gold. I've been sitting on my gold far too long! You too have been sitting on your gold for far too long. It's time to do something.

Start planning. Write down your visions, dreams and goals that you want to accomplish and take it to God. Pray that He send you the right connections. God wants to finance your projects, your dreams. He is a prudent investor. But He wants to see your plan. God will do it for you. He will give you the wisdom to do it. We have the right as heirs of the kingdom, to tap into the wealth, the resources of heaven.

You could also divinely meet someone who will be key to you in fulfilling your destiny or sometimes it will require of you to go to someone for assistance. There is nothing wrong in asking for help. All you have to do is start believing it for yourself. Put aside fear and low self-esteem. Arise and start shining. You have the potential, it's inside of you.

Contend for the Glory of God upon your life and you'll see how you'll begin to excel. God has investment laid up inside of you. It's time for you to pull out that investment and start living to make His name great. I know of people who are holders of high degrees, but are somehow miserable. They have the money, the houses, the cars, you name it. The thing is that emptiness will always be there if you're not connected to your creator God. Accept Him as your personal Savior and be the person God created you to be, to the best of your ability. You can be a doctor and love to sing. You can be a lawyer and love to prophesy or pray for the sick. You know you have the gift, but you're not doing anything about it. Perhaps you bake the most delicious cakes and everyone loves them. Bake cakes and sell them. Can you make lovely pies? Craft things with your hands? Play a musical instrument? Use that gift or talent God has placed inside of you. Satisfaction comes by doing the will of God, by doing what you're called to do.

I always wondered why it is that church people are somehow the 'poorest people' so to say. That is so wrong. We are serving a living, rich God and we're struggling here on earth. We have the mind of Christ, and in the mind of Christ there is no poverty, because that is not His nature. Abraham and other fathers of faith in the bible were rich, because they served a rich God. We serve a rich God. To some the word 'rich' is somehow an offensive thing to say. If you still don't believe that God wants you to be prosperous, why is it that Abraham and the rest of our forefathers were so prosperous? Why is it that they had so much wealth? Where is that wealth today? Are we not serving the same God they served? This is a message for the church to wake up and take a hold of her inheritance. We have an inheritance and we're not even claiming it.

We think holiness is being poor. You need to get rid of such mindsets. No more! Church, we have to take the kingdom by force. It's time to break free from a poverty mindset. It's time to break free from a limitation mindset. Break free from fear! We have everything we need. The church is full of businessmen and women, engineers, designers, doctors, lawyers, you name it. Do something with the gold inside of you. My question to you is; 'When are you going to take action?' Some are waiting on God to talk to them. He's talking all right. He's waiting on you. Go back to school if you must. Take a course, upgrade yourself. Get rid of a man-fearing spirit and take a step of faith. Yes, take that step. You can do it.

You could be a prophet, evangelist or pastor the world has never seen. Your gift will take you places; will cause you to meet people you've only dreamt of meeting. Joseph's gift made room for him. He went from the pit to second in command, in the whole of Egypt.

The sky's the limit if you can begin to trust God from today. Break free, believe and go for more!

Prayer

Father in Heaven, may Your name be lifted up in the Heavens and on earth. You alone are worthy of all the praise. Lord Jesus, I repent for allowing fear and inferiority to control me. Forgive me and set me free. I receive your forgiveness Father. Uproot fear and inferiority and let it be destroyed by fire, in Jesus name. I forgive those who have trespassed against me. I let go of past hurt and pain. I unlock the padlock from my heart and mind, and I choose to soar up into freedom and liberty. I declare I am free. I declare I am whole, in Jesus name.

Amen

Chapter 5

The Glory of God

My desire for the Glory of God started to grow as I read on the life of Moses, Paul and other prophets in the bible. I started studying on the Glory of God. What was it really? I wanted to live in the Glory. As my search for God continued, I had angelic visitations and revelation knowledge on the Glory that was imparted to me that changed my life. I began to see more clearly why God wants us to live in His Glory.

Moses cried out in exodus 33v18;

"I beseech You Lord, show me Your Glory."

That became my new prayer. Show me Your Glory. To live in God's realm, where all things are literally possible.

As I read on the life of Moses, I wondered why he asked God for His Glory. Here was a man who saw many miracles happening and still he too was hungry for more of God. I mean, I'm not even seeing half the miracles he saw. I learned that the Glory of God, is HIS Majesty, HIS Splendor, brilliance, goodness, HIS character and HIS nature. His Glory is 'weighty'. It's heavy. No wonder the priests could not stand when the glory came into the temple. The Glory of God has a lot of dimensions or depths still to be tapped into. Was I living in His Glory? Can I really say that I am experiencing all HIS goodness, HIS nature? Am I living in abundance? Alright, here's the thing. If *part* of the nature of God is Abundance and Overflow, where is that in my life? You're probably asking the same question. Was the main issue really the lack of the Glory of God in my life?

So, by seeking the Kingdom of God is also to seek His Glory?,' I asked. I realized that the Glory of God is also the 'air' of heaven. The earth's air is oxygen. We breathe oxygen into our lungs that causes us to live here on earth. Heaven's 'air' is the Glory. Everything in heaven lives and operates because of the glory of God. We too can be surrounded by heaven's atmosphere. As we pray, read God's word, praise and worship, we get to experience heaven's atmosphere in our sphere.

There are Riches in Glory

The more I pondered on the Glory, the more it dawned on me. I was clearly not living a glorious life. Living a glorious life is living in abundance and overflow of *Glory*. I'm not just talking about a peace in your soul. Oh no, I'm talking about a peace in spirit, soul and body. An abundance of peace, joy, favor, spiritual and material blessings. The nature of God is to bless us in 3D so to say. Not just spiritually. There are however, a lot of us who are only experiencing spiritual blessings. 'Well, I'm happy with just spiritual blessings, this world is just evil, don't want to have material things', I can hear some protesting. That is not a glorious life. I'm not trying to become materialistic here, not at all. I'm trying to see the picture for what it is: The reality rather.

I'm trying to make sense of why God said *'all these things shall be added unto you.'* Where is all the adding God talked about in our lives? Let's be real here. We are living on a real natural planet. Everyone wants to live in his own house and drive his own car right? Yes. But I can also hear some religious minds going, 'but that's not what's important. Loving Jesus and living righteous is more important.' Of course it is. Material things are never to have control over us. Your righteousness is not measured in how poor you are, also not in how rich you are. So we might as well be righteous and blessed materially at the same time. Heaven is a glorious place. It's a place of gold, gemstones and diamonds. God is not bothered by that. In fact, it's His splendor showing off. We will still get to love Jesus for all eternity in all that gold, in all that glory!

Oh yes, and we also get to live in the biggest mansion ever! How cool is that? It's priceless.

Then the Holy Spirit took me to the scripture in Philippians 4v19, we all so love to quote when we need God to come through for us. I know some of you love that scripture too!

It says;

*"And my God will liberally supply (fill to the full) your every need according to His riches **in glory** in Christ Jesus."*

Then it hit me. His riches are **in Glory!** The riches are in Glory! There was a time I prayed this verse. Declared it, shouted it, meditated on it, and prophesied it over my life for a really long time. *The key* God showed me was that I needed to get *in* the Glory. Everything I declared or prayed about was to be declared out of that weighty presence of God's Glory. Things happen faster and spontaneous in the Glory. Riches will be released as you step *into* Glory. The Glory of God is for us, for today. We have to contend for the Glory of God. *The Glory of God is also the realm of God*. Where He dwells. So you cannot be in God's Kingdom and not experience His Glory. You cannot be in His Glory and not experience His riches. The Glory of God is what surrounds Him. He is full of Glory. In fact, He IS Glory! A manifestation of His Splendor, Love and Power! We ought to be full of the Glory of God. The reality is we want the riches of the Kingdom, yet we're not in a "place" to actually experience the riches.

So what happened as I started contending for the Glory of God is that I became aware of the Shekinah or manifest presence of God. That atmosphere or realm where all things are literally possible.

God wants us to live in His realm, in the Glory zone. It all started to make sense as I began to see more and more on how the apostles lived, the prophets and all great men and women. What caused Peter's shadow to heal the sick? It wasn't really his shadow; it was the glory of God that surrounded him to such an extent that the sick got healed by not even touching them.

If you're a struggling pastor, evangelist, prophet or whatever your office, you need the glory of God. That is what's missing in our lives. A lot of things started to make sense as I looked at my life and compared it to the life God wanted me to live. There was definitely a huge gap. How many times have we cried and pleaded with God to give us a breakthrough?

I'm here to tell you that your breakthrough is sure to come as you begin to contend for Him.

There's no effort in the Glory

In the glory of God there is no struggling. Yes, let me say it again. There is no struggling! There is an ease in the Glory.

It goes beyond your gifting. It's the Spirit without measure. There are no boundaries in the glory. There is no distance in the Glory, because there is no time in the glory.

Peter experienced a greater Glory infilling in Acts 4 as they prayed to God to grant them boldness to preach the word. As you read the whole chapter, you'll see how the apostles were persecuted for spreading the gospel. They were accused and thrown in jail. As they prayed in verses 29 through 31, they were all filled with the Holy Spirit. They were filled before on the day of Pentecost, but got filled again with a greater measure in Acts 4. Now that was the key to Peter's breakthrough. It could be your key to breakthrough. I don't want you to miss it. What happened was that the Spirit of Glory came and elevated them to a higher place of Glory. In verse 30 they prayed,

*"While You stretch out **Your hand** to cure and to perform signs and wonders through the authority and by the power of the name of Your Holy Child and Servant Jesus."*

No wonder Peter could walk pass the sick and they got healed. God stretched out *His hand* and healed the sick. This is the desire of every evangelist or minister - to move in such Glory. Peter didn't have to do anything. Talk about an effortless crusade!

Wouldn't it be just wonderful to walk into hospitals where God would just stretch out His hand? It's possible you know.

In the Glory, where you once struggled to drive out demons or just get a revelation, the river flows freely and there is such an ease. Ministry becomes "easier" so to say. Miracles will happen. Blind eyes open up, the deaf hear, the lame walk, body parts literally appear or grow out where they were missing. That is what the apostles experienced. They were ordinary men. If they could walk in that level of Glory, why couldn't we? Imagine two people about to cross a river. One uses a canoe and paddles the water to cross the river. He sweats and puts in a lot of effort. While the other one, uses a motor boat. He just switches on the engine and the boat instead, does all the work. The two people can be compared to two churches. The one struggling to get the anointing and while in that level of anointing gets to see things happening in church, like a few miracles here and there. While the other church, builds up the atmosphere through praise and worship and the glory falls down, they get to see countless miracles, without any effort. Well, where are you currently finding yourself? In the Glory of God or still paddling your way across the river? You choose today how you want to cross the river from now on. It's not a matter of not having the right boat; it's a matter of creating the right boat. All the resources are within your reach, use them.

There's no distance in the Glory

Distance is the length between two places or objects in general. And between these places or objects is time. The earthly realm is limited to a time barrier. It takes time to drive from one city to another, to go to school, your work in the morning or to go pray for someone in the hospital. To go to the bank, stand in line and the list goes on. In the glory, which is the eternal realm of God, time does not exist. 'Well, are we not going to live forever after we die?' Yes, we are. Forever has no time to it.

The ancient Greeks had two words for time, *Chronos* and *Kairos*. Chronos refers to clock time – time that can be measured in seconds, minutes, hours or years. Where chronos is quantitative, kairos is qualitative. It measures moments, not seconds. Further, it refers to the *right* moment, the *opportune* moment. The *perfect* moment. There are no clocks in heaven. I believe we'll have a continuation of special 'moments' in heaven, for all eternity. So to be in the glory, is to experience a kairos moment on earth. The time is always 'right', to do something, have a healing, to sow a seed or have a breakthrough in the glory. You can have kairos moments all the time here on earth.

You can have kairos harvests all the time. Sowing financial seeds in the glory is so powerful. The Lord showed me how our 'financial sowing' *in* the glory is directly connected to breakthrough. Money has become a big issue in the body of Christ. We have developed a mindset of give and it will come back to you. Of course that's what the bible says. But, when nothing happens in a few months' time, or even a year, we complain and stop giving '*our money*' in church. That is an earthly mindset. A Kingdom mindset is 'to give' all the time. To always look for opportunities to give, whereas, an earthly mindset is 'wanting' all the time. Your sowing a financial seed in the glory can have immediate results, almost all the time. Why? Because there is no distance in the glory. The enemy has been fighting this now for decades, and he knows how powerful it is. By sowing a seed, or giving an offering, you are causing sweet smelling incense to rise up to the heavens. You have to understand that in the glory, there is however a fruitfulness. When you sow a seed in heaven, it will immediately grow; it will probably even grow before you sow it. Why? Because of the Glory of God in heaven. That is how fruitful it is in heaven. I don't know if there are any seeds in heaven, but if there are to be any, they will most definitely grow instantaneously! Do you understand the point I'm trying to bring across? Adam and Eve lived in a place where the glory of God was always present.

The Garden of Eden was a glorious place. There was always fruit, throughout the year, food and water. The ground was so fruitful. Everything was just fruitful. There were no struggles in the Garden of Eden. No striving at all. God wants to restore the mindset of the church, the mindset of giving. As you give in the Glory, there is literally no distance and heaven will pour out a blessing upon your land, church, your business and your finances. The key however, is that you got to get *in* the glory. As heaven invades earth, kairos moments are inevitable.

In the book of Acts 8, the angel of the Lord told Philip to arise and go down to the road that runs from Jerusalem to Gaza. He obeyed and met an Ethiopian eunuch. As they encountered each other, Philip ended up teaching him about the word. After some light was shed, the eunuch requested Philip baptize him, *(see Acts 8v26-40)*. Something happened to Philip, as they came up out of the water. Scripture says;

*"And when they came up out of the water, the Spirit of the Lord [**suddenly**] caught away Philip; and the eunuch saw him no more, and he went on his way rejoicing' (Acts 8v39).*

Notice how in a moment's time or suddenly, Philip was caught away and ended up in Azotus. He continued preaching the word of God. Studies proved that to be more than an hour's journey.

How was that even possible to suddenly end up in another city? It was only possible in the Glory as the Spirit of God or Glory came upon him. Please know that nothing is impossible with God. He is looking for a people He can fill with His glory to do great exploits. You are in for the ride of your life as you step into His Glory. It's fun living in the glory. There is much to be experienced. If you don't believe it, it's probably because you need to go deeper. Our earthly mindsets cannot fathom the endless depths of God's Glory.

Carriers of Glory

As a worship leader, I have learned the importance of bringing down His Glory. As worship is a lifestyle to every believer, one has to have a consistency in worshipping God every day. Songs are birthed out of intimacy with God. I tend to write more songs when I'm in worship. In the atmosphere of Heaven, it is just so much easier to write or sing. There are songs yet to be written that have never been sung. Creativity flows in that place of Glory. Every musician or worship leader must cultivate worship on a daily basis. If you're in ministry, you need to be a carrier of God's Glory. Lives will be changed and transformed wherever you go, because the Glory in and around you will make the difference. How then can we be carriers if we are not lovers of the one who is Glory? Get close to the one who is All Glory.

As worship leaders, we need to stand in the River of God to hear the new melodies from heaven. You got to hunger for His presence. How hungry are you? If you're not hungry, ask God to give you a hunger. Ask God to make you desperate for Him. That's what I did, and still continue to do. Whenever I feel like I'm kind of in a comfort zone, I would cry out to God to give me a hunger for Him, for His word and prayer.

I beseech every minister or leader of the Church, to hunger for the Glory of God. Revival is sure to come as the glory of God invades the church. Wisdom will come, knowledge will come. Anything you *need* is in the Glory. God desires for His children to live in His Glory where there is no limitation and no effort. There is definitely more!

Prayer

Lord Jesus, I humble myself before You. I ask that You'll fill me with a greater measure of the Spirit. I hunger for more of Your Glory. Take me higher. Elevate me to a new place in You. Let the rivers of Glory wash over me. Let me breakthrough into the realm of Your Glory! Oh Shekinah Glory, come! Oh Lord, let me be a carrier of Your Glory, in Jesus Mighty name!

Amen

Chapter 6

Holy Desperation

Everywhere on this planet, people are hungry for money, power, fame, love etc. We were created with a void that only God can fill, a thirst that only God can quench. An emptiness that money or power cannot and will not ever be able to fill. Money can buy you lots of material things, yes, but it cannot buy you the love and affection you so crave. You know it's the truth. We all do. That is just a fact, a reality. We are spirit beings, having a soul and living in a body. We were created for God's pleasure. To satisfy Him, worship Him, love and honor Him.

Our young people are seeking love and attention in the wrong places. We grow up in churches where we don't really see much of God's presence. I'm talking about the Supernatural Jehovah God. Young people want to see the reality of the Kingdom. They don't want to just hear sermons on the supernatural and not see supernatural things happening. I'm not saying that serving God is just about seeing miracles and supernatural things. I'm saying that we have been satisfied with a mediocre church for too long.

We are losing our young generation to the world. We need revival. But revival will only come when we get hungry. Are you desperate for change? You see, many want change, but are not willing to sacrifice. When you get desperate, change is inevitable. We all want the anointing, yet we don't want to spend time in prayer. We don't want to go the extra mile; praying in the wee hours of the morning and fasting when no one else wants to. That is the generation we're dealing with. We want the power by the laying on of hands. Just like that. All great men and women of God had to pay a price for the Glory. They had a holy desperation. They cried out to God for revival. They fasted and prayed until something would happen. Moses did anyway. We tend to give up too easily. We want the 'adding', but are not willing to seek the Kingdom first. I want to encourage you to start this journey today by seeking God. God longs for intimacy with you. He wants you to seek Him. And He promises to be found by you. Jeremiah 29v13 says;

"Then you will seek Me, inquire for, and require Me [as a vital necessity] and find Me when you search for Me with all your heart."

Hannah's Desperation

In the 1st book of Samuel, Hannah prayed and was so desperate for God to breakthrough in her life. She was provoked, by her rival Peninnah for not being able to conceive. The two women, to me, are a picture of the church and how sometimes your own brothers and sisters can cause you to feel so unworthy for not prospering in life. It was a hard thing for Hannah not to have any children.

Are you feeling like Hannah felt? Serving God faithfully and not amounting to anything in life? Are you seeing no fruit in your ministry, family or business? Are you frustrated? Then that's a good place to be at. Why, you ask? Frustration leads to desperation.

Year after year, Hannah would faithfully serve God, but there just wasn't any fruit. When was God going to bless her? That could've been thoughts that gushed through her mind as she would see the smile and joy on Peninnah's face. Oh, I know it can be really tough to keep the faith at times, when everyone around you gets blessed and you feel like an outsider. In fact, you even prayed for them and things happened, right? I know the feeling. Then again, you have to rejoice with your brethren for their blessings. You go home and cry out to God, 'When are You going to bless me? When is my time coming?' just to fall asleep again with no answer at times. If you're at a place like this, I encourage you to stay focused. Don't give up yet. God allowed the process of the wilderness to mold and shape you into a better person. Of course He doesn't want you to stay in the desert. Contend for a breakthrough. He will bless you.

Elkanah on the other hand, gave Hannah double portions of the sacrificial meat because he loved her. Well, that was just not what Hannah wanted. She wanted a son from her own loins. She wanted to have her own dream materialize. She wanted her own gift to manifest. Do you have an anointing that everybody acknowledges, but you're just not that financially blessed? Oh you're anointed with double. You pray for the sick and they get healed. You sing and people fall under the anointing. You prophesy and things happen. But all you want now is for your business to get started, or your prophetic gift or ministry that prophets prophesied over you to be birthed. You just want your own son. You just want your own breakthrough.

Hannah's soul was in distress. She came to a place of Holy Desperation. She couldn't take it anymore.

She cried out to her God. She asked for a son and also said that she would give him back to the Lord. Desperation will cause you to make vows to God, holy vows. Remember your vows.

She spoke in her heart, meaning, she prayed from her innermost being. It was a true genuine prayer. Her desperation caused God to visit her. Are you so desperate that God will have no other choice but to visit you? There is something in desperation that causes God to move.

The priest Eli never saw anything like that in his time I believe, as he watched from afar, thought she was drunk. Your desperation may cause others to think you're somehow crazy fasting for 21 or 40 days, or locking yourself in the room for hours seeking God. Whatever it may be, get desperate! Her desperation caused a visitation. Oh and when God shows up, you'll be blessed indeed. God always comes with blessings. It's His nature, His Glory. Frustration births desperation, desperation ushers you into visitation. Jesus may not physically appear to all of you, but when He shows up, whether physically or with His Glory invading your life; it will be a glorious visitation. I have heard countless testimonies from people on how God showed up in their lives after weeks or months of seeking Him. Don't give up, don't quit. God knows when, just keep on keeping on. Hannah knew that in presenting her first fruit to God, He would cause her harvest to be great and to multiply. She knew the principle of sowing and reaping. She knew that to give God her first, God would surely bless her with more. When God comes through for you, what will you do? Will you honor Him with your first fruits or tithes? Will you continue to bless God's people and always cause Him to be number one in your life? Please remember this when things start happening. Always remember God as He remembered you.

Jacob's Desperation

Jacob was known for his deceptive ways, how he tricked his brother Esau, into giving his birthright to him. The birthright was a sacred privilege enjoyed by the first-born son. This privilege made the first-born the real heir and successor to his father, as the head of the family. Jacob proposed to buy the birthright from Esau, he willingly agreed and thus Jacob came into possession of the blessing. After learning the significance of the blessing, Esau later wanted his position back as heir, but it was too late. His father Isaac had already blessed Jacob and it could not be reversed. Esau hated his brother Jacob, he wanted to kill him. After all this drama, their mother Rebekah advised Jacob to flee to Haran (*see Genesis 27*).

Now, after years of living apart from each other, Jacob returned to Edom where Esau lived. Esau journeyed to meet his brother. Jacob on the other hand was in distress. He probably thought of how he tricked his brother Esau and all those emotions came rushing back. He feared that Esau might kill him and started crying out to God. He was desperate for help from Yahweh. He desperately prayed;

"Deliver me, I pray You, from the hand of my brother, from the hand of Esau; for I fear him, lest he come and smite us all, the mothers with the children" (Genesis 32v11).

Jacob didn't know what to expect. He needed a way of escape. Unlike Hannah, he did a terrible thing to his brother. He knew it was wrong what he did. I mean, you probably at times have found yourself in situations where you wronged people, and your heart races at the thought of facing the ones you've wronged. God desires for us to reconcile with man. He wants us to live in harmony with each other. Jacob had to face his fears once and for all. That night Jacob wrestled with God until daybreak, he demanded a blessing. Jacob's wrestling with God meant he was fighting or praying his way through forgiveness, acceptance, love, blessing and breakthrough. Your desperation in prayer is the same. You cry out to God for a breakthrough, for His blessing. Jacob wrestled until God would bless him. He said,

"I will not let You go unless You declare a blessing upon me." (Genesis 32v26(b).

That is the heartfelt cry of a desperate person. If you want God to bless you, 'wrestle' until He blesses you. Remember that this all happened while waiting on Esau. After this all night encounter, Jacob was now to face his brother. It turned out to be a very peaceful reconciliation. Everything worked out great and they were both so blessed to have each other again, as brothers.

The woman with the issue of blood

Here was a woman who had a serious issue, a continuous loss of blood now for twelve years. The bible says, in Mark chapter 5, that this woman tried everything to get well. She spent all her money on physicians, medicine, you name it. She suffered greatly, was weak and just wanted a miracle. She ran out of options. Not only did she lose blood, she lost 'life'. Life is in the blood. Are you finding yourself in a similar situation where you just don't have the strength to go on? Perhaps you are on the verge of a mental breakdown, a marriage falling apart, have children on drugs, you are bankrupt, or you have an incurable disease? This woman heard the reports on how Jesus kept on healing the sick. How he raised people from the dead even. She was desperate for her body to be made whole. Twelve years of suffering has almost left her hopeless, yet, she hung onto a hope that Jesus could make her whole. That's all she had, nothing else. She kept on saying;

"If I only touch His garments, I shall be restored to health" (Mark 5v28).

Everybody there at that time, was pressing upon Jesus. They all wanted to touch him, be around him and all wanted answers to their problems. This woman, however, made her way through the crowd, pushing, pressing and moving forward with the little strength she had left in her body. Finally, when she made it through, she touched Him. Yes, she stretched out her hand and touched His garments!

"And immediately her flow of blood was dried up at the source, and [suddenly] she felt in her body that she was healed of her [distressing] ailment" (Mark 5v29).

Oh my, in an instant, twelve years of pain and suffering just vanished. Not only was she healed, she received her life back, her strength back and her dignity as a woman back. Is there no life in the church where you are serving? Is there a struggle year after year, in your business, your marriage or your finances? It's time to reach out and touch the Lord.

Prophetically, twelve symbolizes Government. This woman had to come out of another government and into the Government of God. Her desperation caused heaven to abruptly come to a standstill.

"And Jesus, recognizing in Himself that the power proceeding from Him had gone forth, turned

around immediately in the crowd and said who touched My clothes?" (Mark 5v30)

Jesus felt power going from Him. He knew, somehow, that there was someone out there who made a heavy demand on His power, someone who touched His Glory. When He asked who touched His clothes, He simultaneously meant who touched His Glory, His Kingdom. The ability of Heaven, the power of God, was gloriously displayed.

Your desperation will cause heaven to turn around and flood you with peace. Peace in spirit, soul and body. You have to become desperate. Desperate people will get to taste of revival. Desperate people will see change. Desperate people will drink from the rivers of Glory!

Prayer

Oh Lord Jesus, I am desperate for more of You! I will not let go of You until You bless me! Hear my cry Oh God!

Amen

Chapter 7

Heaven on Earth

We grew up with the Lord's Prayer, *"Your Kingdom come, Your will be done, on earth as it is in heaven."* What does it really mean for the Kingdom of Heaven to come on earth?

If God said it, then it's possible. Everything God says is yes and amen. How is it that we are not experiencing heaven on earth? 'If it was only that easy', some of you might say. It's not that difficult, it's just that we don't know how. I don't just want to know that it's possible; I want to actually live in that reality. That is the main point here. People tend to tell us a lot of things to do, but they never really tell you how to do it. They'll tell you to stop drinking, smoking, to stop living in poverty, to start this and that, but what we lack is the wisdom to apply it. So if that is the case, we need to ask God for wisdom. He will give it to us.

Jesus, our Lord and Friend, is full of wisdom. He is wisdom. Jesus said to Peter in Matthew 17v27 when they needed to pay their taxes;

"However, in order not to give offense and cause them to stumble [that is, to cause them to judge unfavorably and unjustly] go to the sea and throw in a hook. Take the first fish that comes up, and when you open its mouth you will find there a shekel. Take it and give it to them to pay the temple tax for Me and for yourself."

Being Wisdom Himself, He always knew what to do, how to solve problems, how to get from one side of the river to the other. Well, He just walked on water when there was no boat. Yes, He is Jesus and He can do anything. He can multiply the bread and feed a multitude. He can turn water into wine. He practically lived in heaven on earth. He could bend the rules of physics. Talk about speaking to storms and they obeyed. If Jesus could do that, you and I can do that right? Do you even believe that? If not, believe it. Because He said greater things than this you shall do. If He could open blind eyes, we can command blind eyes to open up. If He could raise the dead, we too can command the dead to rise.

The will of God on earth

As we pray for the will of God to be done on earth as it is in heaven, we ask for His plans and purposes to be revealed and manifested. What then are His plans and purposes? To name a few, God's will is for you to prosper, to be in perfect health, to be saved, to love Him, to preach to a dying world, to live out your destiny, and to love one another. His word is His will. As heaven invades earth, we align ourselves with the heart of the Father, in doing His will.

Adam and Eve were in the will of God, and Adam pleased God by doing His will. He was naming the animals and living out his purpose. You have a purpose. The Kingdom of God is expanded and released as you do His will.

Creating an Eden

The first man Adam and His wife, Eve, lived in the Garden of Eden. Eden means 'delight', a place that was saturated with heaven. Heaven is delightful. God delights or takes pleasure in our worship. Is your home, church or workplace a delightful place for people to come to?

God would visit them and they would have fellowship there and it was just awesome. We all know the story. So as I started pondering on Eden and how they actually lived in absolute abundance and overflow, it dawned on me that, we too can experience Eden. God delights in the prosperity of His children. He wants us to prosper in every area of our lives. He wants us to be in perfect peace, health and lacking nothing. *True prosperity is having the fullness of God in our lives.*

Sin was the cause of their eviction from the garden. But then Jesus paid the ultimate price for salvation, and redeemed everything once again. So wherever you're at, you can start cultivating Eden. Create heaven around you, through your prayer and worship.

True worship attracts heaven and brings down the glory. Your church can be an Eden where others may come and find rest for their souls.

People were drawn to the ministry of John the Baptist, all the way into the desert. Why is that? He was surrounded by heaven. The atmosphere of heaven drove people towards him. Conviction was on his words, piercing their hearts, as he spoke words of life and transformation, which resulted in thousands being saved. Are you preaching and not a soul is responding to any alter call? You need to create an Eden. Are young people leaving the church because they are 'bored'? You need to create an Eden. It's inside of you. A well of glory that can feed a hungry nation that can cause revival to break out. Re-dig the wells of heaven, re-dig the wells of Eden.

Worship Leaders, we need to worship *out* of that place of glory, *out* of heaven as we are surrounded *by* heaven. You can only take people to where you've been. Jesus took Peter, John and James up the mountain of transfiguration. They've never experienced such a thing in all their lives. They had a glorious time seeing the glory of God in such splendor. Peter wanted to camp there. I would've wanted to. Never get stuck at one level of glory. Never camp at a new revelation of the glory or at a glorious experience. Jesus wants us to know that there is always more! There are depths of glory we've never experienced before. You can have heavenly encounters and still hunger for more. The river is always flowing.

Every worship team has a great responsibility to open up heaven over the congregation. If the worship team is dry, they need to get soaked in the glory. There is nothing more frustrating for a minister to preach when there is no glory in the house.

Worship teams, including musicians, need to fast and pray and contend for the glory of God. Musicians tend to think that it's just the singers who need to pray. You have to pray and hunger for God as well. As I teach people on how to play the guitar or drums, I always impart within them the importance of prayer before playing an instrument.

You can be as close to heaven as you want to be. And even as heaven invades this sphere, we have to take up our authority and dominion as Sons of God. We are citizens of heaven.

I like to play the guitar when going to the hospital for ministry, or even just to pray for someone, because even as I sing, the atmosphere begins to change as heaven invades and pierces dark forces. Deliverance and healings are instantaneous. There is an effort as you drive out demons out of your gifting and level of anointing, but effort ceases when heaven invades. When the glory is heavy in a meeting, miracles happen effortlessly. There is just no effort in the glory. Yes, heaven is a prepared place for prepared people. We will go there someday, but God made it possible for us to experience His splendor here on earth. Cultivate Eden in your life. Be a delight to others, as you delight in the God who delights in you.

The mind of Christ

Poverty is a lack of the mind of Christ. It is a lack of heaven on earth. A lack of the Glory of God, because as you live in the Glory, the more of Christ's mind will be imparted in you. Now, I'm not saying rich people all have the mind of Christ. That's not what I'm saying. Like I said before, riches are not just limited to finances, although, a lack of money is a big issue amongst believers. You can have loads of money and still be poor. You can have a rich mind and not have a dime. The thing is where is the balance? Where is prosperity then in spirit, soul and body? We want to experience overflow in all areas of our lives. The mind of

Christ is a mindset of *"All Things Are Possible"*.

It's a mindset of the supernatural and the miraculous. His perspective is completely different from ours. So the mind of Christ in our minds is for our way of seeing or perceiving things to change. To have the mind of Christ is to experience His Glory, His nature, His way of thinking. To think something is to have a picture or imagination. We have to come into His mind so we can begin to see ourselves the way He sees us. The thoughts God has for you are beyond your imagination.

As we see lame or sick people, God sees them healed. Why? Because that's just how the nature of God is. He always sees the end from the beginning. He sees you whole, healthy and wealthy. Because it is *finished*. God always sees the solution. We see the problem. That's why we need to ask for the mind of Christ. Get in the Glory; ask for His thoughts, purposes and plans.

An earthly mindset is full of limitation. An earthly mindset always sees the impossibilities. There is no money, there is no cure and there is no way to get from A to B. While a heavenly, Christ-like mindset is without limits. There is absolutely no limitation in the mind of God. You got to get in the Glory. Cultivate an atmosphere of heaven. Once heaven invades, wisdom comes and you'll know what to do.

What heaven on earth looks like

If I were to go to heaven right now, would I still be wearing these glasses? Would you still have that cancer or incurable disease? Of course not. You'd be whole, complete, lacking nothing and missing nothing. There is no pain in heaven. That was the original plan of God for us human beings, to live a life of bliss. It is available today, as Jesus redeemed everything again through His blood. God wants us to taste of His heavenly splendor here on earth. This may be very difficult for some to grasp, as it has always been a 'striving-to-get by' kind of life for them.

The Father desires for you to be in perfect peace. It is available, but we're still not walking in it. Jesus said;

"Peace I leave with you; My [own] peace I now give and bequeath to you. Not as the world gives do I give to you. Do not let your hearts be troubled, neither let them be afraid" (John 14v27).

As you are surrounded by heaven, you get to experience a peace that is not of this world. Peace in our minds, hearts, relationships, businesses, workplace, marriages, bank accounts. Imagine peace in finances? Where you don't have to worry about where the next bread is going to come from. 'That is a fairytale life, not in this world,' you might say. Well, that's how I used to think, and it got me nowhere. If God said it in His word, I believe it to be true and I want it. We worry too much. We need to be surrounded by heaven. As you spend time in prayer, praise and worship, heaven is sure to invade. Jesus is peace. The more you spend time with Peace, the more peaceful you become. Jesus is Joy. He is Love. He is everything you need. Please bear in mind that I'm not implying that heaven IS already here on earth. I'm emphasizing the fact that we get to enjoy the atmosphere or a glimpse of heaven here on earth. Jesus is the doorway to heaven. There is no other way. Whether you believe it or not, the truth still remains. As Jesus makes His abode in the believer, heaven is real, because Jesus is real.

Whoever said it was impossible? We are the ones limiting ourselves. Stand up and contend for heaven on earth.

Prayer

Lord Jesus, change my mind and heart. Let the mind of Christ be in my mind. Impart within me a blueprint from heaven, on the plans and purposes You have for my life. Surround me with heaven, in Jesus mighty name I pray.

Amen

Chapter 8

Ruling and Reigning

This is a very riveting topic, as it highlights the victorious living of every child of God. First of all, we have to understand what it means to rule and reign. Thus, it is to literally take charge, ownership or possession, also to take authority. We are called to rule and reign with Christ. To rule over circumstances, principalities and also to take charge of our lives.

The bible says that we are seated with Christ in heavenly places. Our seating and reigning with Christ is a position of authority and power. It is to triumph! To be victorious in our day-to-day living. In ministry, our workplace, schools, wherever it may be. It is not a place of failure, depression or defeat.

Joint-seating with Christ is "far above and beyond" all principalities and powers of darkness. Evil spirits can't influence believers who are seated with Christ in heavenly places! This is our inheritance as sons and daughters of God.

Now I know we'll get to rule with Christ for a thousand years and so on, but what we have to grasp is the fact that we get to rule and reign right now, here on earth. Not just someday. Jesus paid the ultimate price for us, and raised us up together with Him and made us sit down together in the heavenly sphere (Eph. 2v6). If that is the case, why is it that we're so beat down, depressed and weary Christians? It's simple, we don't exercise our authority. We don't take charge. We run to people to pray for us every time the pressures of life try to drag us down. I have no problem for people to pray for us, but when are we going to actually realize that we have authority to command storms to subside and to command demons to flee or mountains to move?

Legislating from the courts of Heaven

As children of God, we ought to legislate from the courts of heaven. We have kingdom authority, granted to us by the Father, through Jesus Christ, to make new laws or change existing laws for the purpose of the Kingdom. Only Parliament has the right to legislate on constitutional matters.

The church however, is from a higher government; the Kingdom of God. To be part of the church as Jesus defined it is to be part of a spiritual legislative body tasked with enacting heaven's viewpoint in our society. It is thus not just to go hear a good sermon to keep you for a week. It is also not just to have a wonderful worship experience. Not that all these things are wrong. No. The fact of the matter is, there is so much more to church than just singing, dancing or preaching. Yes, lives are changed every day and that's wonderful and very important, we should however not exclude the fact that we are to *rule* as well. A church doing all that and who knows her position as rulers, is a powerful triumphant church indeed. In the midst of this world filled with sin, corruption, pain, and death, God has placed the church on earth to execute Kingdom agenda.

As joint heirs of the heavenly throne, we get to legislate from the heavens that will affect our governments. Do you know what this means? It means, you and I as the church, have the authority to *rule* and to *overrule*. The church has the right to disagree or disallow of something. So, if the government of a nation proposes to institute a law that is against the Kingdom of Heaven, like abortion or any matter that affects Christianity, that we're against, the church has the authority and power to overrule and change laws. How? Through *prayer and decree.*

Jesus said;

*"I will give you the keys of the kingdom of heaven; and whatever you bind (declare to be **improper and unlawful**) on earth must be what is already*

*bound in heaven; and whatever you lose (**declare lawful**) on earth must be what is already loosed in heaven" (Matthew 16:19).*

If the church is against a new shebeen or pub trying to open up in the neighborhood, we have the power to lock it down in the name of Jesus Christ; to literally stop it from ever opening its doors. Well, if we look around our towns and cities, we see a lot of things we've somehow allowed to happen. The role of the church is saving souls, mentoring disciples, preparing people for heaven, taking care of the widows and orphans and much more. *The purpose of the church, however, is to legislate from the courts of heaven on matters concerning our towns, cities and nation in general; bringing down heaven on earth.* That is the purpose of the church in the Kingdom. To bind whatever is improper and/unlawful on earth and to loose whatever is proper from heaven on earth. Binding and loosing is not to be taken light a thing. It is the authority of the church. It is time for us to take up our authority and Rule and Reign over the Kingdom of Darkness. Not the other way around.

Queen Esther shows us a perfect example of Legislation. As she portrays a picture of the bride of Christ, her 'seat' gave her the authority to overrule. Not only was she called to the Kingdom to finally get out of poverty and lack, but she had a much greater purpose.

Haman convinced the King to destroy the Jews by legalizing a bill where all Jews were to be destroyed. After a three day fast, Esther approached the King in all humility. She petitioned for her people not to be killed. In favour of her, the King granted her request. The bill was averted, made nullified and void. She totally changed a legal law! That is the purpose of the church. (*see Esther chapter 3-8*). We are called to the Kingdom for such a time as this, to destroy and reverse evil plans of the enemy and to institute new kingdom 'laws' from heaven; Righteousness, Peace and Joy. Picture yourself seated with Christ, *in* Christ *in* heavenly places. That is a powerful place to be at.

The problem is not with God, the problem is with us, not knowing our positions in Christ and not exercising kingdom authority. As I started to declare that over my life, my mind changed. The way I perceived things changed.

Principalities are subject to us, they are underneath us. We have a higher rank. They are ruling from the 2nd realm. We are ruling from the 3rd realm, the heavenly realm - the glory realm. Suddenly, you are not afraid anymore. Do you see the importance of living in that realm of Glory? You have to be clothed in righteousness, in Glory. When you cultivate that lifestyle, principalities are not hard to fight. We struggled for years, simply because of neglecting our positions. We did not exercise our authority. We struggled because we were not ruling from that place of Glory.

In every kingdom, Kings and Queens rule by decree.
Job 22v28 says;

"You shall also decide and decree a thing, and it

shall be established for you; and the light [of God's favour] shall shine upon your ways."

Note that *"you"* shall decree a thing and it shall be established. You have to air your voice, to use your tongue for Kingdom purposes.

What are we declaring over our lives, our children, our spouses, our communities, our governments? We have to get our tongues in line with the word of God. Start decreeing. Command Mountains to move, command sickness to go, command money to come, command breakthroughs to come and command divine connections to come for business or for ministry. In Ezekiel 37, God told Ezekiel to prophesy to the bones. The bones were very dry. They were scattered and lifeless. Is your business dry, your marriage dry or your well of finances running dry? Prophesy. Speak life. Decree life in your business; for tenders to come, for doors to open up. What is it you want to see in your ministry? Decree it!

How authority is gained

How do we actually move in that type of authority? Authority is bestowed upon you and is only as good as the person who gave it to you. The higher the authority, the greater your authority becomes. How you gain authority is to come close to the one who is all authority. The closer you get the more authority you have. So, spiritual authority is only as good as your relationship with God. That's why Esther could legislate. She was close to the King. If she was outside the Kingdom or palace, she wouldn't have had that authority. See? Within the Kingdom you have authority, but outside you have no authority. No wonder the sons of Sceva were violently wounded when they tried to drive out demons without any Kingdom authority, (see Acts 19v14-16). The evil spirits didn't recognize their authority, or they probably couldn't see any. They were not clothed in the authority of Jesus. Are you clothed in Kingdom authority? If not, spend time with Jesus. Let Him clothe you.

We have to understand that authority can be lost

through disobedience. In the book of Esther, Queen Vashti lost that authority when she was expelled from the palace. Adam and Eve lost authority when they sinned. They were driven from the garden. Because of their sin, they were stripped from that closeness to God, that authority upon their lives. You have to grow in the authority of God. Jesus came in the authority of the Father and after his death, took back the keys of hell and death, (see Rev 1v18). All authority that man lost was redeemed through the cross. Satan does not have authority over our lives. Jesus said,

*"Behold! I have given you **authority and power** to trample upon serpents and scorpions, and [physical and mental strength and ability] over all the power that the enemy [possesses]; and nothing shall in any way harm you" (Luke 10v19).*

So, for your words to have authority, live in obedience to God and live close to Him. Kings rule through authority, they conquer through power. God wants our words to have authority and power.

The kingdom system functions through and by authority. That's why a decree made by a king has power or 'effect'. Why? Because they rule by decree (authority), and to decree is to authoritatively order. Remember, the closer you are to God, the more authority you have.

Creation and Sound

Let's look at the beginning of creation. God knew exactly how to do it. We read in Genesis 1v2 that, *"The earth was without form and an empty waste, and darkness was upon the face of the very great deep. The Spirit of God was moving (hovering/brooding) over the face of the waters"*

First of all, the Spirit of God was hovering over the waters. The presence of God was present. There was an atmosphere of power and glory for creativity to flow. We all know that God is the source of Glory. There's a principal though to be learned. We have to praise and worship until the glory comes, then out of the glory, we decree. Verse 3 continues to say,

"And God said, let there be light; and there was light".

Notice that *"God said"*. If you start applying this principal to your life, your ministry, business or whatever it is, you'll begin to live a glorious life.

Why is it that by sound He created? He said, *"Let there be light, and there was light."* It's not that God created things out of nothing. He created things out of invisible substance. It was there, it was just invisible. It really intrigued me on why airing your voice is so important. What is it in sound that makes things happen? Sound in the Glory Presence of God?

In every created matter, like our bodies or material objects, are atoms. An atom is the smallest building block in matter. So all matter consists of atoms and any vibrated atom releases sound. Even the chair you're sitting on, or book, kindle or laptop you're holding conveys sound waves. When you throw down that chair, kindle or book, it will release a sound. But in the Glory, you can speak to matter, and it can change form or shape because it can respond to your voice. Now we don't want to go around commanding laptops or books to change form. That is irrelevant. The point is, that words uttered out of glory have a powerful effect.

Creation responds to sound. That's why when you hear music, you respond, whether happy or sad, given the type of music. You feel sad or even cry when something bad was said to or about you, the list goes on. Surround yourself with positive people, prayerful people and worshippers of the living God. We need to go to church and hear the word more often.

In the Glory, words travel at a faster speed and accomplish much more. That's why you can command a person to rise from a wheelchair without touching them, or blind eyes to open up without laying hands on anyone. Why? Because in the Glory there is literally no distance and sound can travel across boundaries. In general, sound travels slower through air, but in the Glory, it is much faster. You can decree a thing without the glory presence and it can take longer, hours, days or weeks even. But decreeing or commanding things out of the cloud of glory, is so much faster. That's how powerful the glory of God is! You can pray for someone in another state over the phone or even in your room and command them to be healed, and it shall be so. Decreeing God's word out of the glory applies to healings, miracles, finances, marriages, relationships and much more. This is a powerful principal to breakthrough.

I had a woman come to me with a request to pray for her marriage. I advised her to create an atmosphere of glory, of heaven, through worship. Then in that atmosphere where the Spirit of God is present in Glory, she must declare whatever she wants done in her marriage. What she wanted to see in her marriage, she must call it forth. After a few weeks, the woman returned and testified about already seeing results. I told her to go back and continue to do so. I myself speak to my body. I would say, 'body, I know you can hear me. I command you to be healed'. Cancer can hear you.

Speak to that cancer and command it to die in Jesus name. I speak to my money, to my hair, whatever it is. For your positive decrees to be effective, you have to first be in the Kingdom, meaning in Christ.

Secondly, you have to get in the glory and speak from that place. There is acceleration in the glory. If you can just begin to grasp this principal, you will live a victorious life!

There's power in your tongue

"Death and life are in the power of the tongue, and they who indulge in it shall eat the fruit of it [for death or life]" (Proverbs 18v21).

You have to be careful what you allow to come out of your mouth. It can be a blessing or a curse. The scripture does say that you will eat the fruit of your words.

Also, don't be discouraged when you positively decree over your life the first time and nothing happens. Keep on doing it. Speak the word. Press through. My prayer life changed. Your prayer life will change. There is a time to pray to God and storm the gates by force, and there is a time to declare.

I literally speak and command things to happen. I exercise my authority every day. Like I said, create an atmosphere of glory through prayer and worship. When the Glory comes down, speak out of that place. You'll begin to see more miracles happen. This is a powerful principal I've learned, and I assure you, it will work for you as well.

God has given us the ability to create. There is creative power available through the Holy Spirit indwelling our innermost being. People get frustrated when things don't innermost being. People get frustrated when things don't happen. Words are like seeds. Seeds germinate when planted in the right 'atmosphere', the soil. It will not grow when you keep it in your hand, on a rock or in your purse, look at it now and then, and expect a plant. No. It will never change form. It will only grow when you put it in soil. Then you have to water it. Words will take form and materialize when decreed from the right 'atmosphere', the glory presence of God. Continue to build that cloud of positive decrees. Sooner or later it is bound to break, and you'll enjoy the rain of blessings.

The Psalmist declared in chapter 45v1;

"My heart overflows with a goodly theme; I address my psalm to a King. ***My tongue is like the pen of a ready writer"***

Write your destiny by decreeing positive things out of the glory realm of God. No one will do it for you. You'll have to do it yourself. You can't continue being negative. Negativity will stop your dream in ever materializing. It is time to take charge of your life, your circumstances. Arise and shine, as the glory of God comes over you. We will only have more when we begin to contend for more of God. Do not be satisfied with your current circumstances, because there is more. God wants us to come to that place in Him where our words will have such power, that even whilst saying it, things begin to happen. That is the life we're called to live. Joshua commanded the sun to stand still, (Joshua 10v12), Elisha cursed young lads that mocked him and bears immediately devoured them, (2 Kings 2v23-24), Jesus commanded demons to flee and they obeyed. There are countless accounts in the bible where words had dynamic affect when uttered.

It is clear that the solar, animal, demonic, earthly and all kinds of realms are subject to us. For we are seated high above, in the realm of Christ.

Living an ascended life

Being seated with Christ in heavenly places is to live a life of ascension. It is also to live in the *cloud* of Glory. As a church, we have been stuck at merely 'resurrection'. Resurrection is great. We get to be alive and we move in a greater power. There is more though, Ascension. Jesus, after His glorious resurrection, ascended into the heavens.

"And when He had said this, even as they were

looking [at Him], He was caught up, and a cloud received and carried Him away out of their sight" (Acts 1v9).

A cloud of glory ushered Him into the third Heaven where He is seated at the right hand of God the Father. We are seated with Christ, in Christ. Living an ascended life is to live a 'royal/throne life'. Living a throne life is to rule and reign.

Being caught up in glory every day is the life we are called to live. God's desire for the Israelites was to live in Canaan, a place of milk and honey. We think that Canaan is merely limited to having a job, earning a six figure income, driving 10 cars, living in the biggest mansion. No! Material things are not your promised land. The Promised Land is to live in the Glory - heaven on earth. Of course it will result in financial breakthrough, but being blessed is not just having material things.

The blessing is to live an ascended life, in the glory, full of the glory of God and being seated with Christ in heavenly places here on earth. Ruling and reigning out of heaven on Earth, the Glory Zone. I realized that the Kingdom of heaven, the Kingdom of God is actually our promised land. Jesus was our forerunner. He paved the way for us. To some, this would probably be very difficult to grasp, because of the way you grew up spiritually. The Kingdom of God will turn you upside down, or rather, 'right-side-up.' You'll find religious stuff

coming out of you, as you're being transformed. The Pharisees couldn't understand the Kingdom system. It messed them up big time. They were used to a pattern of religiosity for centuries. As He went around, Jesus' purpose was to bring the Kingdom here on earth.

You can read this book and just say it was another good book, or you can start implementing it. It's your choice. I would really want you to make the right choice. I would love for you to excel in life.

To live a purposeful and victorious life. There is so much more for you. Take a hold of it now!

Prayer

In the name of Jesus Christ, I decree and declare that I am a wealthy, healthy, prosperous, loving, kind and giving person. I declare I'm anointed and live in the realm of Glory. I declare I am the righteousness of God, an heir to the throne. I am royalty! Right now, I command the heavens to open up and release an inundation of blessings in my life! Every storm, I command you to be still in Jesus' name! Circumstances, you will change, you no longer have a hold on me! I rule over you. I rule over sickness, disease and poverty. I command you to leave my life in Jesus name!

Amen

Chapter 9

A Supernatural Life

I believe living a supernatural life is to live above and beyond natural. This world is natural. We are not natural. We are supernatural. Why? Because we are not just human beings living a spiritual life, but we are spiritual beings living a temporal life as a human. That's why a lot of Christians find it hard to live a supernatural life. They are so bound to this world and its desires, that they forget why they're actually here. We are to live above sickness, lack, poverty, depression and oppression.

The Supernatural is an eternal realm. This earth is temporal, like your body. Our spirit is Eternal. To have a supernatural life is to live beyond and above the limitations of this world. The Holy Spirit at work within us will do super-abundantly, above all that we could dare ask, think or imagine, (Eph. 3v20).

We are powerful supernatural beings, created by a Powerful Supernatural God. It does not mean that you get to be weird now. The reality is that as you pursue God with all of your heart, your life becomes a habitation for God. We have to be surrounded by glory 24/7. Not just when we pray or worship. To always have that flow of wisdom and knowledge, peace, joy and love. That is a supernatural life.

An open Heaven

An open heaven can be described as an opening or portal, where God localizes His glory or presence over the life of an individual, church, city or nation in outpoured blessings and power. It is the manifestation of heaven on earth. It is possible to live in an open Heaven that is what we call, *revival*. The inundation of blessings, power, favor, you name it.

It is our responsibility as a church to keep the heavens open. How? Through righteous living, prayer, praise and worship.

Angelic visitations, dreams, visions, revelation knowledge and prophecies are all characteristics of an open heaven. I started having dreams and visions on specific things. I saw an increase in visions and dreams and revelation knowledge. I had angelic visitations I've never had before. It must be the desire and heart-cry of every minister to have an open heaven experience. Apostle Paul was caught up into the third heaven (2Cor 12v2). He had supernatural encounters. Abraham had supernatural encounters. Jacob, Joshua, Mary, Elizabeth and lots more, had supernatural encounters. Jesus himself had supernatural encounters. The heavens opened when He was baptized. He lived and walked under an open heaven, all the time. Open heavens are not just for some people. They are for all His children, but only those who hunger and seek Him in spirit and in truth will get to walk under it. The heavens were also opened when Stephen was killed as the first martyr.

"But he, full of the Holy Spirit and controlled by Him, gazed into heaven and saw the glory (the splendor and majesty) of God, and Jesus standing at God's right hand; And he said, Look! I see the heavens opened, and the Son of man standing at God's right hand!" (Acts 7v55,56).

At this, the members of the Sanhedrin covered their ears screaming and rushed upon him, stoning him to death. Religious spirits will always resist an open heaven. Of course the enemy does not want us to live in an open heaven, because he knows what will happen. He knows that a church living in an open heaven is a dangerous, powerful church. His works will be exposed and destroyed, that's why he doesn't want you to pray. An open heaven is marked by a significant increase in the spirit of prayer and worship.

The enemy doesn't want you to fast and seek the face of God, he doesn't want you to worship your way into heaven.

Peter, falling into a trance, saw heaven opened and something like a large sheet being let down to earth by its four corners *(see Acts 10:9-23)*.

Through this open-heaven revelation, the door opened to the Gentiles. Peter was shown he was not to declare unclean what God had declared clean. A whole new chapter of God's purpose for the earth began.

You too can receive revelation that can change a generation. So many great things await you if you can just begin to believe for a greater glory. If you're not yet saved or born-again, accept Jesus Christ as your personal Lord and Savior. You too can have a supernatural life. It awaits you as you decide to embark on this journey you were created for.

Wealth Transfer

As you live a supernatural life, God's desire is for us to be in wealth.

"The Lord shall open to you His good treasury, the

heavens, to give the rain of your land in its season and to bless all the work of your hands; and you shall lend to many nations, but you shall not borrow" (Deut28v12).

In the glory, the season is always right for blessings, because it's a fruitful atmosphere. Heaven's atmosphere, the glory, is always ripe with blessings. It's a one big, long continuation of fruitfulness and blessings. As heaven invades your life, ministry, church or business, wealth is sure to come. Why? Because Jesus' glory is His goodness, His nature; the fullness of Who He is. He can't help but bless us. Be reminded that in heaven, there are no seasons. So whenever the glory show's up in your life, your *'season'* shows up. So, living in the glory is to always live in season – on earth. Because the glory is one big *season* of *'spring'* - joy, peace, happiness, blessings, you name it!!

When we are living under an open heaven, not only is the Spirit outpoured, but we can often also experience increased financial blessing. How do we maintain that flow of blessings? By always creating an atmosphere of glory. Stay and live in God's glory.

Wealth is not just limited to finances, although spiritual outpouring can signal increased financial outpouring, but there are riches in Glory yet to be transferred.

Anointing's, power, mantles, inventions, ideas, revelation and much more, are some of the riches or wealth God has in store for the church. The wealth is for Kingdom purposes. Under an open heaven there is though such a fundamental inner change that material things have no hold on us. In obedience to the Spirit, they can be released for the benefit of the gospel. We can therefore be trusted with substantial material increase.

You are probably already experiencing great financial wealth. What are you really doing to expand the Kingdom of God? Are you just gathering for yourself, or are you actually supporting the work of the Kingdom of God? Know that as God blesses you, you ought to give. Find someone, a church or an outreach organization and start blessing them. Help others make their dreams come true. Do something for someone else.

Dreams and Visions

To dream or to have a dream is to hear from God whilst asleep, while visions are received while awake and they are often 'in the Spirit'. Dreams and Visions are the language of the Holy Spirit. Now, I'm talking about real Godly dreams. Yet, it is possible to have dreams and visions from another source, when you are not in the Spirit. Be continually plugged into God, the true source of revelation. As heaven opens up, there will be an increase in prophetic dreams and visions. Write down your dreams and visions. Pray and ask God for correct interpretation. We need to contend for a breakthrough of the revelatory realm.

The Prophet Joel did say;

"And afterward I will pour out My Spirit upon all flesh; and your sons and your daughters shall

prophesy, your old men shall dream dreams, your young men shall see visions" (Joel 2v28).

Let's look at a few biblical accounts where real life people had dreams and visions that changed their lives.

Joseph's Dream

In Genesis 37:5-8 it says;

"Now Joseph had a dream and he told it to his brothers, and they hated him still more. And he said to them, Listen now and hear, I pray you, this dream that I have dreamed: We [brothers] were binding sheaves in the field, and behold, my sheaf arose and stood upright, and behold, your sheaves stood round about my sheaf and bowed down! His brothers said to him, Shall you indeed reign over us? Or are you going to have us as your subjects and dominate us? And they hated him all the more for his dreams and for what he said."

Joseph's brothers hated him even more for this dream and his father Jacob rebuked him for it, but this dream was prophetic and later came true in Joseph's life. After his brothers sold him into slavery, he later became second in power over Egypt and his brothers actually did bow down to him.

Jacob's Dream

This dream is recorded in Genesis 28:12-14 where,

"He dreamed that there was a ladder set up on the earth, and the top of it reached to heaven; and the angels of God were ascending and descending on it! And behold, the Lord stood over and beside him and said, I am the Lord, the God of Abraham your father [forefather] and the God of Isaac; I will give to you and to your descendants the land on which you are lying. And your offspring shall be as [countless as] the dust or sand of the ground, and you shall spread abroad to the west and the east and the north and the south; and by you and your Offspring shall all the families of the earth be blessed and bless themselves."

God stood at the top of the ladder as Jacob's perspective was changed concerning his assignment. This dream was also prophetic and would later come true. This dream has been realized today because Abraham and his sons have descendants in both the Arab world and in the nation Israel.

Ezekiel's Vision

In Ezekiel 1: 1(b)-3, Ezekiel records;

"The heavens were opened and I saw visions of God. On the fifth day of the month, which was in the fifth year of King Jehoiachin's captivity. The word of the Lord came expressly to Ezekiel the priest, the son of Buzi, in the land of the Chaldeans by the river Chebar; and the hand of the Lord was there upon him."

John's Vision

In the Book of Revelation, John recorded,

"I, John, your brother and companion (sharer and participator) with you in the tribulation and

kingdom and patient endurance [which are] in Jesus Christ, was on the isle called Patmos, [banished] on account of [my witnessing to] the Word of God and the testimony (the proof, the evidence) for Jesus Christ. I was in the Spirit [rapt in His power] on the Lord's Day, and I heard behind me a great voice like the calling of a war trumpet" (Rev 1:9-10).

Once again, we see that this vision is from God as he was "in the Spirit." The Book of Revelation is not the revelation of John but is actually the "revelation of Jesus Christ", which God gave him to show to his servants the things that must soon take place. He made it known by sending His angel to his servant John" (Rev 1:1).

Like the dreams, this vision was prophetic. Visions in the Bible were always from God.

Some people say, 'there is no need for new visions and dreams anymore, everything is already in the bible.' Well, just like the people of the bible walked with God, we are in a living relationship with our Creator God. Why would God not want to talk to us today?

"For God [does reveal His will; He] speaks not only once, but more than once, even though men do not regard it. [One may hear God's voice] ***in a dream, in a vision of the night, when deep sleep falls on men while slumbering upon the bed"*** *(Job 33:14-15).*

We quickly dismiss our dreams and visions as unimportant, when in fact; God may have sent us a message. God sends messages to us in dreams or visions in order to protect us from impending disaster, change a lifestyle we've been living, or perhaps guide us in a direction to take. God is concerned about us. He is our Father. Abimelech was admonished in a dream about committing adultery with Abraham's wife, Sarah. But God came to Abimelech in a dream one night and said to him;

"Behold, you are a dead man because of the woman whom you have taken [as your own], for

she is a man's wife" (Genesis 20:3).

Through this dream, Abimelech repented and changed his ways. God will also guide you through dreams. He did it for Joseph (Mathew 2) and for Pilate's wife (Matthew 27:19). Sometimes God gives you a dream to simply encourage you. For example, when Gideon needed reassurance to fight the Midianites, he was inspired through a dream and its interpretation. Gideon arrived just as a man was telling his comrade a dream. *And he said;*

"Behold, I dreamed a dream, and behold, a cake of barley bread tumbled into the camp of Midian and came to the tent and struck it so that it fell, and turned it upside down so that the tent lay flat. And his comrade replied, "This is nothing else but the sword of Gideon son of Joash, a man of Israel. Into his hand God has given Midian and all the host. When Gideon heard the telling of the dream and its interpretation, he worshiped and returned to the camp of Israel and said, Arise, for the Lord has given into your hand the host of

Midian" (Judges 7:13-15).

A lot can be said on Dreams and Visions. What is important is to stay connected to God. If you're not really much of a dreamer, that's fine. Not everybody will have prophetic dreams or have vivid visions. And if you're a dreamer, don't think less of others because they don't have the 'gift' like you do. But, if you really want to have God speak to you through dreams and visions, there's nothing wrong in asking. Ask and it will be given you.

While some are dreamers, others may have knowledge, wisdom, discernment of spirits, prophecies, miracles, signs and wonders or angelic encounters. Well, these are the things you can expect in an open heaven. Living a supernatural life is meant to be exciting and fulfilling. Throughout the bible, we see various accounts where the heavens opened up and lives were drastically changed.

Keys to unlocking the Heavens

So what can be done to open the heavens? A lot of things can be said on this, but the most important to remember, is to always first start with repentance. Repentance is the *first golden key* to opening the doorway to heaven.

"If My people who are called by my name, shall humble themselves and pray, and turn from their wicked ways, then will I hear from heaven, forgive their sin, and heal their land" (2 Chron 7v14).

God promised to hear from heaven if we repent and turn from sin. Your land could be your body, your marriage, your business, your ministry, whatever it is. If you're not treating your spouse with the necessary love and respect, repent and change. Is it perhaps your employees that you're not treating fair? Repent and change. What about secret sins no one knows off? Well, whatever it is you know is against the will of God, repent, change and be a better person. God promises to heal your land, only if you submit to Him, repent and turn. Be righteous at home, church, work, school, when no one sees you, everywhere. Righteous living attracts the heavens.

The *second golden key* is fasting and prayer. Fasting is all about God, getting closer to Him and being humble; there are however benefits to fasting. I have learned over the years and have seen that fasting is a powerful key that literally puts 'speed' on answer to prayer. Sometimes, it is important to fast and pray as it breaks down strongholds and opens the heavens wider.

The *third golden key* to unlocking the heavens is through praise and worship. Praise and worship ultimately brings down the glory of God. It is so much effective to worship with a clean heart, to lift up holy hands to a Holy God. Praise and worship touches the heart of the King and moves Him to Tabernacle amongst His children. While prayer stacks the throne, praise and worship *releases* the throne. When God moves in, heaven moves in. You have to understand that praise and worship is all about Jesus. It's not about us. We are not doing it to merely 'feel' good. We are doing it because it pleases the King, also to show our adoration and love for Him.

The *fourth golden key* is tithing. God promised to open up the storehouses of heaven, to open up the windows of heaven for you. I would like to emphasize that without tithing, the windows of heaven will never open over your life. Now this is not to condemn anyone, it is just a reality. Tithing is a command from the Lord, and when we're not obedient the heavens are shut.

Imagine using all four keys at the same time. It will definitely have a 'nuclear bomb' effect. Yes, there might be more than four keys, but these are already a great start. Keys have been given to us to unlock whatever is in heaven. Sometimes we pray and ask God to open doors for us, whilst He is waiting on us to use the keys. Everything is already there, use the key God has placed in you.

The Supernatural awaits as you unlock the heavens by faith. Faith is to take action. Faith is what pleases God. So start unlocking.

Prayer

Lord Jesus, launch me into the Supernatural. It is Your desire for me to live a Supernatural life. I want to walk under an open heaven. Let Your Glory rain down on me, in Jesus name!

Amen

Chapter 10

It's all about Jesus

In the light of all that has been said, I would like to emphasize the fact that Jesus must and always should be our number one love. Do not get so caught up in the Kingdom that you don't spend time with the King anymore. The key to everything is intimacy with Jesus. It is imperative for us to really know and understand it.

Loving Jesus

What does it really mean to love Jesus? We must first define what is meant by the word *love*. Since we are discussing Jesus, we will limit our definitions to the two primary Greek words used for "love" in the New Testament. The first is *philia*. This refers to a brotherly love, or to a close association with another person. To demonstrate this type of love would not require any substantial sacrifice on the part of the lover. This love is shown through a cordial attitude and an allotment of time. Anyone, mother, brother, sisters, colleagues, friends, can be loved with *philia*. This type of love will easily fade, that is, if the loved one moves away or is not often encountered. This is not the type of love that would be adequate for the kind of love Jesus wants from His followers. The other Greek word for "love" is *agape*.

This is love that is considered unconditional. This is the love that Paul describes in 1 Corinthians 13 and is most appropriate for understanding what it means to love Jesus. Paul explains this type of love by what it does and what it does not do.

According to 1 Corinthians 13:4-8, *agape* is patient, kind, rejoicing with truth, bearing all things, believing all things, hoping in all things, and enduring through all things. *Agape* does not envy, boast, or rejoice in wrongdoing; it is not arrogant, rude, selfish, irritable or resentful. Most importantly, *agape* does not end. It will not fade away like *philia*. *Agape* is not based on circumstances and will never end. Agape is eternal. It is not a temporal thing, or an emotion that can quickly just die when somehow, I didn't get what I wanted. That is true love, although, often times, we still really struggle to fathom the depth of this love. To love the Lord is to follow Him wherever He leads, to obey Him whatever He asks, and to trust Him whatever the circumstances. To love Jesus is to reflect the love that God has for us.

"In this is love: not that we loved God, but that He loved us and sent His Son to be the propitiation (the atoning sacrifice) for our sins" (1 John 4:10).

Do we really obey Him in whatever He asks? Do we really trust Him? If not, we need to ask God to give us that love for Him. Also, it is all based on relationship. And to have a relationship, is to spend time with God. The reason why we probably don't trust Him enough is because of a lack of time spending.

To love the Lord is to care for the ones He loves. It saddens me, when I see how cold we've become towards one another. Everyone is just for himself. We don't really care anymore. What happened to looking after the widows and orphans, the needy and poor? 'Well, that is just not my calling', you might say. Does it require for one to be called in that field to care? You find someone sitting next to you in church, with barely shoes on, or a suitable dress, and you turn a blind eye. If we really love Jesus, we will begin to extend a helping hand to the needs of others. You don't have to feed the five thousand now, I'm not saying that. Start with one person. Don't wait on God to show you or talk to you specifically, He already have. It's in His word. It's possible to give without loving, but it's impossible to love without giving. Are you willing to give your heart, soul and everything, even your possessions to Jesus as you surrender to Him?

'Everything, yes, but just not my possessions', some might say. We really don't want to go there.

It's funny how, in the beginning, when God comes through for us, we say, 'God, this is your house, car, job', but after a week or so, we are reluctant to offer someone a lift from church or to church. We complain and moan, when the pastor asks for a donation, or love offering to buy instruments or to attend to a need. It is time for us all to make a thorough investigation of our own lives.

Agape is not based on emotion but on the will. You hear people say things like, 'I'm just not feeling like it, or, 'I don't feel like praying or reading the bible, going to church nor doing something for Jesus right now. Well, you need to 'grow up' in love. Feelings are subject to change. You feel like this now, later you feel different. Our soul must be soaked in the love of God's fire.

When Jesus said,

"If you [really] love Me, you will keep (obey) My commands" (John 14:15).

He was teaching that loving Him would be a demonstrable action, not an emotional feeling. If Jesus is to be loved as He commanded, then a conscious choice must be made to act according to 1 Corinthians 13. To love Jesus is to willfully act in such a way, that our devotion to Him is proved through our actions toward Him.

Loving Jesus when it hurts

Throughout the years of my Christian life, I have learned that the key to a triumphant life is to love Jesus when hurting. We live in a world where we are not exempt from heartache and pain. A supernatural life does not mean you'll never experience trouble. Trouble is everywhere, yet having Jesus is what makes the difference.

We are not alone in this world. We have a helper, the Holy Spirit who helps us overcome every obstacle in life. Whenever I find myself in situations that are heartbreaking, I worship my way into healing love. I have found that running to another source of comfort is not the answer. Running to Jesus and worshipping Him, soothes the pain and eventually lifts you up out of unpleasant emotions. I always tell people that whatever you go through in life, the key is to run to God and not away from Him. Running away opens a door to disaster. It pleases the enemy when we try to find solace in worldly places. Your breakthrough lies in loving Jesus while it hurts. Worshipping Him while in pain; Jesus is our healer. As you stay in the secret place, healing grace will overwhelm you and saturate you. It is the best place to be at when hurting.

I have a friend who lost her husband due to an accident. It was a terrible time of ordeal and distress. I have watched this young widow friend of mine find solace in God. At times when emotions rage and it feels too hard a thing to bear, she would cry out to God. It was and still is a journey of healing for her as she worships God, loving Him with all her heart. Some, however, run to alcohol, drugs or other worldly pleasures in hope of finding comfort. Only Jesus can heal a broken heart, only true Love can. Worship Him in times of anguish. He promised to never leave you, never forsake you. He is always close, closer than a brother.

Passionately pursue and love Him. Be a relentless lover. Go to that secret place and seek Him. He is waiting for you, longing, to take you away with Him. There is more, but can only be found in Him. Jesus is saying, *'come up higher, my love, come up higher'*. There is so much more awaiting you. Step into reality! Step into Love.

Godly Encounters

All throughout scripture, encountering Jesus changed the lives of people. Abraham, Moses, Paul, the Samaritan woman and lots more, changed when they had God encounters. An encounter with the King changes everything.

Queen Esther's life changed after encountering the King. Your life too can and will change.

It was in a time of fasting and prayer that I had an outpouring of the Glory of God. I've had angelic visitations since and dreams that altered my destiny. It was in these visitations that I received revelation and impartations of fire, love, anointing and a visit to heaven. My whole view on angels and heaven changed, as I got to see them for the first time. There is something in "seeing" that changes you.

As you seek God, He will show up in your life. And when He does, it will shake you up, in a good way. What happened to me was merely the grace of God. It doesn't make me extra special, it can happen to you as well. In the end, it's all about Jesus. It's all about encountering the King of Kings. He is the center of it all. He is our satisfaction. He sustains us, day and night. Being with Him, in His presence is what satisfies. Living in His Glory, satisfies. Loving and being loved by the One who is *All Love* is satisfying.

We have to pursue the one who created us. We have to hunger for an encounter, but most of all, press on for a habitation of the Most High - Yeshua Hamashiach.

Surely, there *is* more!

Salvation Prayer

Dear God in heaven, I come to You in the name of Jesus Christ. I acknowledge to You that I am a sinner, and I am sorry for my sins and the life that I have lived; I need Your forgiveness. Lord Jesus, I forgive those who have trespassed against me. I believe that Your only begotten Son Jesus Christ, shed His precious blood on the cross at Calvary and died for my sins, and I am now willing to turn from my sin. You said in Your Holy Word, Romans 10:9 that if we confess the Lord our God and believe in our hearts that God raised Jesus from the dead, we shall be saved. Right now I confess Jesus as the Lord of my soul. With my heart, I believe that God raised Jesus from the dead. This very moment I accept Jesus Christ as my own personal Savior and according to His Word, right now I am saved.

Thank you Jesus for Your unlimited grace which has saved me from my sins. I thank you Jesus that your grace always leads to repentance. Therefore Lord Jesus, transform my life so that I may bring glory and honor to You alone and not to myself. Thank you Jesus for dying for me and for giving me eternal life.

Amen.

Begin by praying and if you need to forgive others, do so with the help of the Holy Spirit.

Welcome into the Kingdom of God the Father, Son and Holy Spirit.

BIBLIOGRAPHY

Greek Time (McKinley Valentine)

The four loves (C.S. Lewis, 1960)

The Amplified Bible (© Zondervan, 1987)

www.ingramcontent.com/pod-product-compliance
Lightning Source LLC
Chambersburg PA
CBHW060533100426
42743CB00009B/1515